UNFILTERED GRACE
BELIEVING THE WHOLE GRACE MESSAGE

JOE LANGLEY

Easter Press

Published by

Easter Press

www.EasterPress.com

Unfiltered Grace
Believing the Whole Grace Message
© 2014 by Joe Langley

Unless otherwise noted, Scripture quotations are from THE HOLY BIBLE, NEW INTERNATIONAL VERSION®, NIV® Copyright © 1973, 1978, 1984, 2011 by Biblica, Inc.® Used by permission. All rights reserved worldwide.

Scripture quotations marked (NLT) are taken from the Holy Bible, New Living Translation, copyright © 1996, 2004, 2007 by Tyndale House Foundation. Used by permission of Tyndale House Publishers, Inc., Carol Stream, Illinois 60188. All rights reserved.

Published in North Fort Myers, Florida by Easter Press

ISBN 978-1495303579

For speaking engagements and ministry information, you may contact the author at:

www.UnfilteredGrace.com

www.DrJoeLangley.org

@DrJoeLangley

CONTENTS

CHAPTER ONE

GRACE... MADE TO FIT

I don't think I've ever met a Christian who did not believe in grace. We depend upon it. We thank God for it.

Congregations sing about it. The hymn "Amazing Grace" is probably the world's most well-known hymn as it continues to top the lists of Christian favorites. And I imagine most Christians can recite Ephesians 2:8: "For it is by grace you have been saved, through faith."

So we sing about grace and we talk about grace and we know that we are saved by grace.

As I said, I have never met a Christian who did not believe in grace.

But I have met many Christians who wonder if they are worthy or adequate in God's eyes. They fear they are falling short of measuring up to God's standards for acceptance. While still believing in grace, they also believe that God's opinion of them is shaped by their own works and their own righteousness.

I've met preachers (and I have been one myself) who preach about grace but then outline what Christians need to do to stay right in the eyes of God. They will declare the wonders of grace, but then in the same sermon exhort their hearers to manage their sin and to strive in their own human strength and dedication to please God.

And I have met Christians who feel great guilt about their attempts to live godly lives. They come to church to

1

discover ways to deal with that guilt – even if they are made to feel even more guilt before they leave the church service.

I know of Christians who are serious about the call to holiness. They strive to do all the right things in their desire to please God. Church attendance, daily quiet times, serving on church committees or ministry teams and all the other expected spiritual activities are followed faithfully. They do these things because they want to – but they also do them because they are supposed to. And although they would never admit it (for it would be a sin), they become judgmental and condemning of others who are not as serious or as dedicated.

I have also seen people give up because they just can't do it anymore. They genuinely tried but they can't live the life they hear commanded and now the struggle has worn them out. They got tired of the whole thing and chose to get off of the spiritual treadmill.

I know people who were excited about their new-found relationship with God, but the rules of religion soon robbed them of the joy. Their initial awareness of God's acceptance was replaced with a list of expectations necessary to stay in God's good favor.

I have also seen people walk the aisle again and again to rededicate themselves. This time they are serious. This time they will try harder. And when they walk the aisle a few weeks or a few months later they remake that same commitment. Only this time, they are truly serious!

I have even known people who have been baptized multiple times because the other times evidently did not take. They consistently fell short of what they were supposed to be or to do. They just didn't live up to the standard and so they got saved and baptized again.

But every last one of them believes in grace.

2

Why is there this disconnect? How can people love grace but not accept it? How can they speak of grace but not rest in it? How can they believe in it but not apply it?

Part of the reason is the standard message they are hearing in the pew and reading in many Christian books. That standard message has the theme of sin management in which they learn to control and overcome their sin. They hear that it is up to the serious Christian to discover and deliver on what pleases God.

Another part of the problem is that many Christians have a limited understanding of grace. They believe that while grace is the gateway to our salvation, good works are the path we are then called to follow. No conflict is seen between this mixing of grace and works. What do we believe and trust that God expects of us in order to be saved? Faith in the work of Christ and reliance upon Him. But what do we then say that God expects of us in order to be pleasing to Him? Works that *we* accomplish and a reliance upon human faithfulness. And there is no conflict sensed between those two ideas.

Jesus saw a conflict. He said the new way and the old way could not be mixed. It would be like putting new wine into old wineskins (Luke 5:37).

The Apostle Paul saw a conflict. He said that the two could not co-exist. They nullified each other.

> And if by grace, then it is no longer by works; if it were, grace would no longer be grace. (Romans 11:6)

But the prevalent message being taught and being heard today does not see the conflict. Many Christians believe it is a little of both: God calls us to accept His grace but we must still strive to please Him.

3

This tension between the teachings of grace and the emphasis on good religious works does not create a conflict because many Christians pass everything they hear about grace through the filters of past teachings and personal understandings. Our sermons and hymns and Bible study lessons and Christian "how to" books are so full of the combining of grace and works that people comfortably accept both. We make them fit. We sense no conflict in saying "Grace, but..." or "Grace and..."

I have had people nod their heads as I spoke of the joys of grace living, but then in the very next moment minimize it by mixing it with law. And I have read Christian best sellers that speak of grace as the only way God deals with us, but then on the very next page outline the demands for legalistic works.

How can this be?

This occurs because of those well-established religious filters. The Grace Message is modified and balanced out so that there is not a conflict. We can nod our heads to grace but still hold onto a works mentality. Grace just has to be filtered down a little. But when it is filtered down, it becomes only a shadow of its whole. The bigger picture is missed.

The full picture of grace cannot be contained in a simple definition. Grace is so much more than the amazing mercy of God extended to us at salvation. Grace is God doing for us what we cannot do ourselves. It is His *God*ness responding to our *human*ness. Grace is the way God has chosen to relate to us then, now and forever. It describes the way God viewed us and loved us when we were His enemies in our minds; it is the way God operates in our daily lives and empowers us now; it is the way God judges us and forever looks at us through the perfect righteousness of Christ. Grace

4

is about Jesus. It is about who He is. It is about what He did. It is about His finished work. It is about what He is doing. But it is not just *about* Jesus. Jesus *is* Grace.

What would happen if we allowed grace to be grace? What if we removed all the religious and man-created filters and considered the truth of God's pure grace? What if we didn't diminish or take away from God's grace? What would happen if we accepted the Biblical teachings about grace at their face value? What if we were to believe the whole Grace Message?

We would first have to understand what the Bible says about grace and what it says about law. An understanding of unfiltered grace has to begin there.

CHAPTER TWO

THE LAW: GOOD OR BAD?

The Law was bad, but it was good. Or, maybe it was good, but it was bad.

Actually, it was both.

The Law was good because it outlined moral and ethical instructions for individual lives and for society. The prohibitions and directives were worthy instructions that outlined how man was supposed to live. Law established a framework for society. But it was bad because it demanded a standard that no one could consistently attain. If the Law was to be the standard for righteousness, it would prove to be an unattainable standard.

So it was bad since no one could live up to it. Even after man's best efforts, it could not bring about righteousness in God's eyes. Instead it only brought condemnation. In some instances it brought about false pride. But it never brought real righteousness.

But it was good because it did exactly what God designed it to do. God did not miscalculate. He gave the law for a purpose.

So, was it bad or was it good?

God was the originator of the Law. And everything God designs and creates is pleasing to Him. So obviously it had to be good. But that is true only when we realize and accept God's actual purpose for the Law.

6

A Consistent Result

It must have been an awe-inspiring experience to go up on the mountain top to communicate with God, but from the day that Moses brought the Law down from the mountain it hasn't worked out very well for man. Man tried and failed and repented and tried and failed again. The story that begins in the Garden of Eden and runs throughout the Old Testament is the record of mankind's failure, consequences, and repentance only to repeat the cycle again. The problem was not with the law; the problem was with the law keepers. Or more accurately, the law attempters.

That cyclical pattern has been consistent since the beginning and it remains true today. Law still does not provide a way to righteousness. It never has and it never will. But it did accomplish exactly what God designed it to do.

God's Purpose for the Law

People are often surprised when they discover what the Bible actually says about the purpose of the Law.

It is most typically seen as a measurement of how well we are following Christ. It tells us how to be good. We hear it defined and stressed and held up as the standard we are to attain. The Law is framed and hung on the wall; some want it hung in our courthouses and schools. We are taught that adherence to the Law is the mark of a faithful Christian.

In reality the Law has always had only one true purpose. *God designed the Law to show us how desperately we need a Savior.* This is what Paul clearly expressed in his letter to the Galatians. He said the role of the Law is quite different from what we have most typically heard it to be:

Is the law, therefore, opposed to the promises of God? Absolutely not! For if a law had been given that could impart life, then righteousness would certainly have come by the law. But the Scripture declares that the whole world is a prisoner of sin, so that what was promised, being given through faith in Jesus Christ, might be given to those who believe. Before this faith came, we were held prisoners by the law, locked up until faith should be revealed. *So the law was put in charge to lead us to Christ* that we might be justified by faith. Now that faith has come, we are no longer under the supervision of the law. (Galatians 3:21-25, italics added)

The Law was never intended as a possible way to righteousness, but rather was designed to lead us to Christ. It was to show us that we cannot do it on our own and that we need a Savior. That was God's purpose. He designed it to prove that righteousness could never be attained by man's performance and obedience. God knew that man had to try it his own human way before he would accept the only actual way. So God designed the Law to make us conscious of our sin and our need for a righteousness from God apart from the Law. That righteousness was given in grace through faith in Christ.

Therefore no one will be declared righteous in God's sight by the works of the law; rather, *through the law we become conscious of our sin.* But now apart from the law the righteousness of God has been made known, to which the Law and the Prophets testify. This righteousness is given through faith in Jesus Christ to all who believe. (Romans 3:20-22, italics added)

Paul says that the Law and the Prophets (with their calls for obedience) were actually just making the point and were part of the process. No one could ever become righteous by keeping the Law. But God knew that. The Law was given to prove that point. Righteousness could only come another way.

An overview of the full Bible teaching reveals that the Law has always had only this one actual purpose. God designed the Law to show us how desperately we need a Savior. The Law was not a failure if it is seen in its intended purpose. It was actually very successful for no one can debate that it reveals a need for another route to righteousness.

Righteousness had to be accomplished some other way. That was always God's plan.

A Definition of "The Law"

It might be helpful to have a fuller definition of "Law". The Law definitively outlined rules that specified whether certain behaviors were right or wrong. It gave the standard. By implication it judged whether a person's conduct was good or bad. And the Divine laws determined whether a person had right standing or righteousness with God.

The first Divine law was given to Adam and Eve when God commanded them not to eat from one specified tree. The failure of law was revealed very early because not only was that command the first law God gave man, it was also the first law man violated.

Other laws were given on other occasions. Then, when the nation of Israel was on the way out of slavery in Egypt and headed to the Promised Land, God gave Moses what we know as the Ten Commandments. These ten laws were clear and precise. They addressed our relationship with God and with one another. For good measure, God inscribed them on two tablets of stone.

The Ten Commandments soon became the cornerstone of all religious law. Stipulations were added to the original Law as they were defined and supplemented by more laws to help man keep the original laws. The original commands were eventually expanded into over six hundred rules and regulations. The majority were negative: "Don't do this." Some were positive: "Do this."

The Law began to govern how far you could walk on the Sabbath Day. Directions were given as to what size stone you could pick up and lift on the Sabbath without violating the command to keep the day holy and free from man's laboring. One of the more amusing new stipulations was that a woman was not to look in a mirror on the Sabbath. Why? She might see a gray hair that she would pluck out. That would constitute working on the Sabbath!

By the time of Jesus' earthly life and ministry a religious leadership group called the Pharisees was responsible for interpreting the Law for the people. Numerous laws continued to be added by their design. By this time in spiritual history, "righteousness" and "keeping the Law" had become synonymous.

How does "Law" look today?

"Law" is any standard that gauges a person's right standing with God. It is any rule that one keeps in order to become more holy or more pleasing to God. This attitude and insistence upon obeying the Law creates a system of sin management. In truth, it is legalism. No one wants to be described as a legalist, but it is a common perspective in many Christian churches.

Legalism bases our relationship with God upon *our* actions and *our* work. How do you know if someone is a legalist? There is a simple test. Ask the question, "What do we need to do in order for God to be pleased with us?" If the answer is anything other than "Believe in Christ", then the person has added a legal list to his Christianity.

That question is based upon the most basic definition of a legalist. A simple definition of a legalist is a "person who has a legal list." Legalism always has a growing list of what we should and should not do. It is the list of performances that we believe God expects.

Legalistic rules today specify acceptable levels of church attendance and support, appropriate behavior, style of dress, frequency of reading the Bible, various types of unacceptable activities to avoid - the legal list goes on and on. To be even more confusing, different churches have different lists. Some lists are longer and some lists are shorter. But the reason for the lists is always the same. Legalism defines the standards.

The problem occurs when someone believes that by keeping certain laws he can affect his relationship with God. The implication is that legalistic obedience will affect God's attitude towards him. He concludes that his own works of obedience are the measure of God's approval. Man makes himself the initiator of righteousness as God is reduced to the role of a responder.

This is the message of the majority of sermons and teachings we hear from religious Christianity today. It is logical. It is measurable. It allows us to maintain a certain level of control. It makes sense. But it is exactly opposite of what the Bible teaches.

Paul's Gospel and the Truth about Law

The man traveling the dusty road between Jerusalem and Damascus was unwavering in his devotion to God. But recently, a group of heretics had been speaking of a new way to God that was by faith in the recently crucified Jesus of Nazareth. And that's why the man was rushing towards Damascus. His name was Saul, and he was going to imprison the devotees of those blasphemous teachings.

But his journey was interrupted by the intervention of a blinding light and a voice from heaven. That Damascus encounter would result in a new man, a new mission, and a new name. And Saul the enemy of the gospel became Paul the chief proponent of the new way of righteousness.

The Apostle Paul was a major legalist... before he met Christ. He identified himself as such in Galatians 1:14.

> I was advancing in Judaism beyond many of my own age among my people and was extremely zealous for the traditions of my fathers.

The Apostle continues to recount that he received his gospel by no one other than the Spirit of God. He did not consult with any man. He didn't even visit the initial disciples in Jerusalem. His gospel and his message of grace were the results of a direct revelation from Christ Jesus. This is the gospel that he spoke of in Romans 1:16.

For I am not ashamed of the gospel, because it is the power of God that brings salvation to everyone who believes.

Later in the following chapters of Romans, Paul outlined the key components of his gospel. And where did he begin? He began by talking about the Law. Having been a Jew and a student of the Law his entire life, he now had received a new understanding of the role of the Law.

Condemnation through the Law

Paul taught his readers that the Law did not control and prevent sin, but it did serve to make men aware of their sin.

> "Therefore no one will be declared righteous in [God's] sight by observing the law; *rather, through the law we become conscious of sin.*" (Romans 3:20, italics added)

The Apostle said that the intention of the Law is not to govern behavior, but it is to identify our own inability to achieve righteousness. Law does not prevent or remove sin; it makes us conscious of the sin in our lives. Depending upon the Law to do anything else has a serious result. The Apostle reveals this in Galatians 3:10.

> "All who rely on observing the Law are under a curse."

We are commonly told that the Law is good and beneficial. It needs to be followed. In fact, most Christians believe that it needs to be taught in our churches, our schools and throughout society. But Paul said it was a curse and that all who rely upon it were under that curse. Why would he say that?

Paul understood that whenever the Law was stressed, condemnation always occurred. Always. Every time. It never results in true righteousness. Instead, the Law always brings condemnation. It can do nothing else for that is what God designed it to do!

A faulty concept of this designed purpose results in a harmful misunderstanding. We might think that God will be pleased by attempts to adhere to His Law, but the only points scored with God by following the Law are negative points. It is a curse. It is a ministry of condemnation (2 Corinthians 3:9). The condemnation produced by relying upon the Law always leads to one of two unfortunate directions.

Sometimes the result of attempting to live by law is a condemnation of self. A lawbreaker feels guilty because of his sin. He promises himself that he will stop a particular sin. He then promises God. And he really means it. Sometimes this takes place in the privacy of his prayers. Sometimes it occurs while kneeling before a church altar with tears rolling down his cheeks. But one thing is absolutely certain: he will repeat that sin again. So he begins to feel despair. He feels like a spiritual loser and knows that God must be greatly disappointed. Now, in even greater despair, he rededicates and recommits only to find himself soon again asking forgiveness for the same sin. For him, the Law's commands and requirements have become a curse and a condemnation – just as God designed it. However, the lawbreaker doesn't understand that this is what is supposed to be. He sees himself as a failure without seeing the way of hope.

Other times the condemnation created by the Law leads to a condemnation of others. Have you ever noticed how we judge others by their actions, but we judge ourselves by our intentions?

While some people look at their own sin and they feel failure and guilt, some people look at the sins of others and feel a pride in their own self-righteousness. This self-defense mechanism allows them to justify and rationalize their own sins. They are the spiritual descendants of that prideful Pharisee who thanked God that he was unlike the sinners around him.

God designed the Law to be a condemnation, but His purpose was that it would be a condemnation of our own efforts at righteousness. He never intended it to be a point of comparison. And He never intended that the Law would be a pathway to pleasing Him. But He did plan for the Law to have a positive result.

He intended that the condemnation created by the Law would show us clearly our need for a different righteousness. His designated plan for the Law was to condemn our own efforts at self-earned righteousness. He knew that there would be no clear designation of sin without the Law. And He knew that there would be no awareness of our need for a Savior.

Many times in today's religious contexts, the Law is used to motivate human behavior, but ultimately that approach always fails. This is because laws might temporarily manage and control behavior, but they cannot change the root cause of the behavior. Stressing obedience to laws will not produce consistent results. It was never designed to do so, and it never will be successful at doing so.

Let's say that we are concerned with the promiscuity of teenagers. How can we motivate them to remain sexually chaste until marriage?

A typical strategy is to stress the rule and tell them it is wrong. We can show them that this is God's rule. We can explain that when they engage in premarital sex, they are sinning against God and they are violating His plan for their lives. Perhaps we could have them make a pledge to God and themselves. For extra measure let's have them make that pledge in front of a church congregation. Will that work? Let's also give them a ring to wear on their finger so they will be continually reminded of their pledge.

All these ideas sound like a promising plan and it has been utilized by many churches. Yet all follow-up surveys show that this strategy has no long term effectiveness in reducing the percentages of teenagers having sex. So the common response by the concerned adults is that more emphasis and more teaching are needed about the rules. But rules don't affect behavior unless there is strict monitoring. And even then they still do not work effectively. They certainly do not work consistently.

But this never was God's prescribed way to achieve holiness and righteousness. A rules-based godliness can never be effective. That's why there had to be another way.

CHAPTER THREE

RELIGIOUS BEHAVIOR MODIFICATION

A legalistic emphasis on God's rules or man's rules is nothing more than behavior modification. But does it work?

It can address behavior on a surface level if there is the acknowledgment of a need to change and if there is a genuine desire to change behavior. But even then there is a constant struggle to not fall off the wagon and revert to the harmful behavior. But to get beyond modifying behavior on a surface level, one has to get to the root cause and the root source.

Psychologists sometimes attempt to take people back to a point in life that is thought to be the root basis of their current behavior. That is often helpful as we understand the development of dysfunctional behaviors that impact families and individuals.

But the problem with religious behavior modification is that all humans have a deeper root cause. We all have a human nature that makes us act like humans. The Bible teaches that our human nature is also a sin nature.

I like the joke about a preacher who bought a used lawnmower he found in the classifieds of a newspaper. The seller advertised that it started easily, but the preacher was unsuccessful the first several times he attempted to start the mower. He immediately contacted the seller. "Well," he was told, "You have to cuss at it." "What?" the preacher replied. "I don't know how to cuss." The former owner answered, "Just pull that cord for five to ten minutes. It'll come to you."

I've never met anyone who had to be taught to sin. It's not a necessary instruction because we all have a human sinful nature. Proper behavior can be defined and confronted, but that sin nature cannot be overcome with any consistency.

But God did not give the Law to modify our behavior. He gave it to show us that a new righteousness is necessary.

Why do people follow laws?

I was recently laughing as a friend was telling his experiences as a highway patrolman. He told me that he would sometimes drive along five to ten miles per hour under the speed limit just to see how long the other drivers would reduce their speed. He chuckled as he remembered that he seldom got passed.

Those drivers were demonstrating one of the main motivations people have for following laws. They fear the consequences that they might experience if they break the law.

The *Dallas Morning News* recently reported that a woman in Dallas was arrested because she had $76,039 in fines for running through toll booths without paying. This total had been accrued by going through the toll entrance 2,953 times. There was also a $25 administration fee for each violation. A toll-way spokesman said that they realize some people don't have the correct change or might get in a wrong lane, so they allow drivers one or two violations without contacting them, but they do go after repeat offenders. My first response was to wonder how many people will now drive onto the toll road once or twice without paying. They've just been told that infrequent violations of the law have no consequences. And when you remove the consequences, our human nature loses a motivation for obeying laws.

We saw this same motivation expressed when Hurricane Katrina unleashed its fury in September 2005. Reporters and camera crews caught individuals robbing businesses and homes of valuables. Some even caught looters leaving stores carrying big screen televisions. One of those caught by a TV camera crew in New Orleans was asked, "Doesn't it bother you to do this? Don't you know it's wrong?" The looter's response was insightful, "If it is wrong, then why aren't the police here to stop us?"

We probably find that attitude appalling, yet at the same time many Christians obey God because it is a law and we fear the consequences of not obeying.

Another motivation for obedience is that we fear disappointing someone of significance in our lives. We want our mothers and our spouses and our pastors to be pleased with us. We might adapt our behavior if we know they might find out about our actions and be disappointed.

Closely aligned with this desire is our concern for our reputation. We sometimes have the presence of mind to stop and consider what a sinful behavior will make our church or family or community think of us. But this is often circumvented when we have an awareness that no one will ever know. This motivation is also minimized when we are in private or out of town or when we don't believe we will get caught.

These motivations (fear of consequences, desire to please, concern with reputation) have a direct connection to our reasons for obeying God. We don't want God to punish us by making our hot water heater go out or by causing our car to break down. And of course, the biggest fear is losing our salvation and being condemned to an eternal punishment.

We want to please God. This is a good desire, but it is impossible to please a perfect God with our behaviors no matter how well we might match up to others. And, to top it off, we hear that He is constantly watching over us. It is no surprise that one of the most common perceptions of God in today's society is that He is a *Policeman in the Sky* watching to catch us when we sin. Or, God is much like Santa Clause; He's making a list and checking it twice to find out who is naughty and nice.

Laws require increasingly stricter restrictions to cover the failures.

Laws, by their very own nature, require additional definitions to guarantee that the original law is suitably obeyed. That's why the ten becomes the hundreds.

Remember the childhood story of the little boy who tried to stop the dike from leaking by placing his fingers into the holes? The only problem was that he soon ran out of fingers. A new hole kept popping up.

The Law is like that leaking dike.

Laws for righteousness don't have a final line. There just isn't any final scale. Someone keeps adding to the fine print. This alone should make us realize that we need a more effective guide than a list of do's and don'ts. But we just keep adding to the list.

Christians need to understand God's designed role for the Law. One can rightfully argue that it did have a behavioral purpose. Its guidelines provided a basis for order and served as the foundation of a society. But spiritually the Law was

UNFILTERED GRACE

given to make man conscious of his need for a righteousness that he could not attain in his own efforts. The Law was not effective for producing righteousness; the Grace Message teaches that God has offered a new way that is.

Living by law will never produce true righteousness.

Here again is the greatest problem with the Law. Living by a standard of adherence to the Law cannot result in righteousness. The Bible is clear on this point.

> "... no one will be declared righteous in his sight by observing the law." (Romans 3:20)

It is difficult to read any other interpretation for Paul's statement. He is clear that no one will ever be able to attain a righteousness by his own obedience. The failure rate is one hundred percent. And yet we continue to set ourselves up for failure. We want to obey the Law because we want to live righteous lives. But the Biblical truth is that living by law will never produce a life of true righteousness. It simply cannot. It never has. And it never will.

A Practical Implication

This understanding of God's intent of the Law directly refutes all ideas of living a certain way in order to affect our standing with God. But if it is an approach guaranteed to fail, then why is it so widely emphasized in today's churches?

The majority of teaching in churches today is focused on sin and upon preventing sin. We go to church to hear sin

21

defined and specified. We are taught to avoid it. We go for correction. This almost universal message is that we are to employ a sin management approach.

The sin management approach identifies sins. It teaches that sin is bad and God is good. Therefore, since we sin, we are bad and should feel guilty. This creates a need to hear preaching and teaching that reveals and reminds us of our sin. Repentance and confession are constantly necessary to restore us to right standing with God. As one pastor once told me, "We need good work at the altar."

But that moment of forgiveness is a brief moment because we soon sin again. So, the cycle is continually repeated as we attempt to manage and control our sin.

The rationale for this approach is understandable. Some people receive a catharsis from having a defined process to deal with their guilt. It also allows us to maintain a personal sense of control; we are responsible and in charge of handling our sin.

In spite of its popularity, the result of the sin management approach is a treadmill that wears us out emotionally and spiritually. Christians who whole-heartedly agree that human effort cannot bring about our salvation - we depend on Christ alone for that - fail to understand that it is not human effort that keeps us righteous in God's eyes.

Ezekiel is considered one of the most significant Old Testament prophets. He understood and proclaimed that the true definition of righteousness was perfection. He exhorted the people of God to abide by the Law. But Ezekiel also discovered the problem of attempting to achieve righteousness through the Law. He concluded that righteousness by works comes and goes.

"Therefore, son of man, say to your people, 'If someone who is righteous disobeys, that person's former righteousness will count for nothing. (Ezekiel 33:12)

What was Ezekiel saying? He revealed that true righteousness by the Law does not work. People can follow the Law time after time, but if they fall short in just one instance, their previous righteousness counts for nothing. They are unrighteous in God's eyes. Ezekiel hit upon the reality. Living by a standard of adherence to the Law cannot result in righteousness.

So is the Law good or bad?

The Apostle Paul was a spiritual mentor to the younger Timothy. Our Bibles contain two of the letters that Paul wrote to encourage and guide his young friend whom he often referred to as his son in the faith.

Paul wanted Timothy to understand the true relationship between law and grace. His first letter to Timothy includes just a few brief comments before Paul gets to his key point.

We know that the law is good if one uses it properly. We also know that law is made not for the righteous but for lawbreakers and rebels, the ungodly and sinful, the unholy and irreligious... (1 Timothy 1:8-9a)

Paul taught that the Law served a good and valuable purpose. But that was true only if it was used properly to lead to the correct conclusion. It was never intended as a way to earn righteousness. No, it was intended to show lawbreakers the need for choosing a new approach.

Holding on to that Legalism

The man sitting in my office across from me had requested a meeting. I had just begun to preach a more focused grace message that was difficult to run through the religious filters. The man asked me, "Why are you so against a focus and adherence to God's Law?" I'm glad it had become that apparent.

But I am sympathetic to Christians ensnared by legalism. I know very few insincere legalists. They have to be serious because their approach requires a high level of dedication and commitment. But the danger is that it often results in pride. (See the Pharisees of Christ's time for exhibit A.) Or, it sometimes results in frustration. Either way, it doesn't work.

I recently saw that man who questioned my concerns with legalism. Ten years have now passed and he remains hard on himself as he strives to please God and earn His full acceptance. Sadly, he doesn't know that he has already received it. He expressed to me a hope that God will forgive him for some missed opportunities to witness. Additional things have happened in his personal life that have created other failures in his legalism. But he is still trying.

He believes in God's grace but he doesn't understand that grace and legalism cannot co-exist. He doesn't realize that they were never intended to do so because each one negates the other. He still believes that Law and morality and good deeds are significant components of the way to righteousness. In seeking to be true to God, he has missed

God's truth to him. He has missed God's intended purpose for the Law.

CHAPTER FOUR

A NEW WAY

One of the definitions for "sin" in the Bible is "missing the mark." That is the literal meaning of the Greek word (*hamartia*) which is translated as "sin" in most English translations. It is the word picture of an archer not hitting the center point on the target.

I can identify with that! The lone success I experienced the one and only time I attempted archery was to make the arrow fly towards the general direction of the target. Hit the mark? Not even close.

If the Law is an impossible standard of righteousness to aim towards, then what hope do we have for righteousness? Don't we all miss the mark?

After writing in Romans 3:20 that no one can achieve righteousness from obeying the Law, Paul continues on to speak of a new way of righteousness. He wrote that it was a different path to righteousness.

> "But now a righteousness from God, apart from law, has been made known, to which the Law and the prophets testify." (Romans 3:21)

God always knew that man could never achieve righteousness by the Law. That's why the Law's only purpose was to make us aware of our sin. Righteousness had to come another way because a righteousness through the Law didn't work. Everyone misses the mark. We might conclude that humans are inconsistent in their ability to behave righteously. Actually we are very consistent! We never can consistently hit the mark.

We choose to become Christians in large part because we realize the need for forgiveness. We are aware of our sinfulness and we recognize (or fear) the spiritual consequences. So we accept God's offer of salvation. We are forgiven! We are new creations in Christ Jesus!

But then after that salvation experience, we continue to have a desire for righteousness. We keep shooting at the mark. We believe that our righteousness is the basis of God's judgment. We hear that godliness leads to rewards. We are told that it is our way of pleasing God.

But the Bible says that God-pleasing righteousness does not come from the Law. That's why we need a righteousness apart from the Law. We need another way. A way that works.

Can't It Be Both?

It is very common to mix the new way of righteousness, which is apart from the Law, with the righteousness that is by the Law. But that is like mixing oil and water. It doesn't work, but that has never kept man from trying.

This mixing has been occurring since early Biblical times. Old Testament writers promoted an earned righteousness while at the same time recognizing the futility of that effort. The attempts seem surprising in the contradiction.

In Psalms 119:7, the psalmist speaks of a man's sincere desire to live according to Law and religious regulations.

> As I learn your righteous regulations, I will thank you by living as I should! (*New Living Translation*)

But later, in Psalms 143:2, the reality of the situation becomes clear.

> Don't put your servant on trial, for no one is innocent before you. (*New Living Translation*)

Do you see the discrepancy? On the one hand, there seems to be a sense that righteous living is a possibility. The readers are encouraged to learn of God's righteous regulations and then to live as they should. But then twenty-three chapters later in the *same* Old Testament book the reality hits home with the admission that no one is innocent of breaking God's laws.

This same contradiction is later presented by another Bible author. This writer also spoke of the blessings of living by God's righteous Law.

> The righteous lead blameless lives; blessed are their children after them. (Proverbs 20:7)

But he too later realized the impossibility of such an attempt at righteousness. His genuine desire was followed by an awareness of failure.

> Indeed, there is no one on earth who is righteous, no one who does what is right and never sins. (Ecclesiastes 7:20)

It might seem difficult to see that this is the same author writing these conflicting statements. How can he say that the righteous live blameless lives but on the other hand say that there is no one righteous? Surely this could not be the same man.

But it is. Both statements were written by wise King Solomon.

What about the Ten Commandments?

Don't the Ten Commandments detail a way of righteous living? Don't they tell us what God requires of us? Aren't they clear in their teaching?

Again the Bible shows the futility of mixing law and grace. Paul writes in 2 Corinthians 3:7 that the ten laws that were engraved in letters on stone "brought death." He called them a ministry that brought condemnation.

The Apostle consistently makes the point that righteousness can never come about by Law. Here are just a few of his statements:

As it is written: "There is no one righteous, not even one;" (Romans 3:10)

Therefore no one will be declared righteous in God's sight by the works of the law; rather, through the law we become conscious of our sin. (Romans 3:20)
For if a law had been given that could impart life, then righteousness would certainly have come by the law. (Galatians 3:21b)

What is more, I consider everything a loss because of the surpassing worth of knowing Christ Jesus my Lord, for whose sake I have lost all things. I consider them garbage, that I may gain Christ and be found in him, not having a righteousness of my own that comes from the law, but that which is through faith in Christ—the righteousness that comes from God on the basis of faith. (Philippians 3:8-9)

Paul says that righteousness by Law and righteousness by faith are two separate ideas. If the first one had worked, then there would be no need for the second. We have to choose. And we can't choose both.

They don't mix.

What did Jesus say?

The crowd was gathered at the designated place on the designated day. It was the Sabbath and each man was at his place in his synagogue.

According to the custom of the day, any teacher or rabbi could stand in front of the crowd and read from a scroll of the Old Testament writers. But there was still a noticeable stir when the man, Jesus of Nazareth, stood and chose the scroll containing the writings of the prophet Isaiah.

News about this Jesus had been spreading. His authoritative teachings in other synagogues were being praised. He was already earning the reputation of one who spoke with knowledge and insight.

Now as Luke records in the fourth chapter of his gospel account, Jesus stands to speak in a synagogue in His own home town. This might not have been Jesus' first sermon, but it is the first one for which we have any details.

The crowd was quiet with anticipation as He unrolled the scroll and began to read:

> "The Spirit of the Lord is on me,
>   because he has anointed me
>   to preach good news to the poor.
> He has sent me to proclaim freedom for the prisoners
>   and recovery of sight for the blind,
>   to release the oppressed,
>   to proclaim the year of the Lord's favor. (Luke 4:18)

He then calmly rolled up the parchment and returned it to its place. But it was the next words coming from His lips that created a buzz among the people assembled.

> Today this scripture is fulfilled in your hearing. (Luke 4:21)

This first recorded sermon foretold what would be the repeated emphasis of Jesus' teachings. But read the full story. You will find that He never visited any prison or opened any jail doors to allow the inhabitants to run free. Neither would He have much success in converting the religious and self-righteous. He would confront them and address their false sense of righteousness, but they would never be His focal audience. His audience was the hearers who did not believe they were righteous.

They were not imprisoned by stone dungeons or iron shackles. Instead, they were imprisoned by the prevailing religious system that demanded righteousness by observing the Law. They were oppressed by the demands of legalism. And Jesus had come to set them free.

Matthew also records Jesus' intent and focus.

But go and learn what this means: 'I desire mercy, not sacrifice.' For I have not come to call the righteous, but sinners." (Matthew 9:13)

Jesus did not come to reinforce and uphold the system of Law and sacrifice. He did not come to affirm those who were comfortable with their own righteousness. Jesus did not come to mix mercy and sacrifice. And He did not come to combine grace and law.

But Jesus did come to bring hope to those who were aware of their need for God's mercy. He did come to offer a new means of salvation to those who knew that they were sinners.

The Old Way Did Not Work

The testimony of the Old Testament writers. The teaching of the Apostle Paul. The message of Jesus. They are all in agreement. It is confirmed.

No one could ever attain righteousness by observing the Law. No one could make himself righteous in God's eyes.

Imagine a courtroom. You are seated at the defendant's table for you are the one on trial. Accuser after accuser makes his way to the witness stand. Each one confirms the charges against you. As each witness recites the same condemning evidence, the deserved verdict becomes clear. You are guilty. You are not righteous just because you did many righteous deeds. No, you are found guilty by that legal system because you violated many laws. You broke many laws when it only took one violation to make you a lawbreaker.

In spite of your best intentions and your best efforts, you have fallen short. Your guilt is unquestioned. You need a different way to receive righteousness. You need a new way.

That New Way

The word *gospel* means *good news.* The gospel is *glad tidings.* The angels chose the word to express the news of joy announced to the shepherds in the field outside of Bethlehem on the night of nativity. The apostle Paul selected the word to summarize the message that he unashamedly proclaimed.

What was this good news? What were these glad tidings?

> For in the gospel the righteousness of God is revealed - a righteousness that is by faith from first to last, just as it is written: "The righteous will live by faith." (Romans 1:17)

The good news is that a new way of righteousness has been revealed. It is a righteousness not achieved through works or Law, but it is gained by faith. Man was given the Law through Moses, but grace and truth would come through Jesus Christ (John 1:17). He would bring a new way to righteousness.

This righteousness would not be earned as a reward for being obedient to the Law. No, it would be given to all who believe (Romans 3:22). God would give it in His grace. And it would be a true righteousness and holiness (Ephesians 4:24). It would be a righteousness and a holiness fully satisfactory to God.

This righteousness would be given apart from the Law. It would be given through His grace. And it would be a new righteousness that is to be accomplished in a new way.

Which approach?

The talk about Moses and the Law, the Pharisees and self-righteousness, Jesus and the gospel, and the new righteousness from God all fit neatly into our understanding of the New Testament. But how does it relate to the Christian messages we hear today?

Even though we agree that the Law could not produce righteousness, we still focus on an approach to righteousness that is based on managing and controlling sin in our lives by our own efforts. We define the guidelines and seek to follow those guidelines. We continue to ask God for His forgiveness when we don't follow the guidelines. We rededicate ourselves to doing better.

This pattern repeats itself again and again.

The message we continue to hear in religious circles is that message of sin management. We want to know what we are expected to do. We want to be reminded of what we are not supposed to do. The focus is on controlling and overcoming our sin.

But as we saw earlier, the Sin Management Road to Righteousness continues to lead only to one of two results.

It leads to self pride as we compensate for the unrighteous things we do by focusing on the righteous things we are doing. It is a comparison game. I look at me and I look at others. I excuse my shortcomings and I condemn the sin I see in others. I am thankful that I am not as bad as other sinners.

Or, sin management leads to despair. We can fool others, but we cannot fool ourselves. There is a sense of guilt and failure. We try but we just cannot. So we try harder. We desperately desire God's acceptance but realize deep down that we are not doing all that is necessary to merit it.

Each one chooses his own road

There are two different roads that men take to reach righteousness. We can choose the road of good works and self-righteousness or we can take the road of depending wholly upon having the righteousness of Christ imputed to us.

We can't mix the two for they do not follow identical paths. Actually, they are opposite roads heading in different directions. And they never intersect.

A few pages earlier in this book, we were in a courtroom in which we were found guilty. If we have heard many sermons at all we have most likely also heard an additional illustration for that final day in God's court that Christians will experience.

God is on the judge's seat and we are on trial. But Jesus is our defense attorney. Satan is the prosecutor. God declares us guilty but Jesus goes forward to pay our fine.

I think there is a more accurate illustration that is more aligned with the truth of grace. The commonly told version misses that truth.

God is the judge, but we are not the ones on trial. We are not in the defendant's seat. It is Christ who is being judged. He is the one sitting in the seat. And God declares Christ to be righteous because of His sinless life and His sacrificial death.

We are seated in the gallery. And God now addresses us. He declares that Christ's righteousness has been given to us. He has chosen to take our sin and place it upon Jesus. Our guilt has been removed. And the righteousness that Christ has attained? God the Judge declares that He is crediting that righteousness to us.

> God made him who had no sin to be sin for us, so that in him we might become the righteousness of God. (2 Corinthians 5:21)

And so we have a choice to make. We can strive for a righteousness by works. Or we can receive the righteousness of Christ. We are to choose one of those two ways. We can't attempt both for they negate one another.

We can only pick one.

Chapter Five

Salvation or Righteousness?

A realization of the vital importance of this new way of righteousness becomes more evident as we consider what happens to a person when he is pardoned at the moment of his salvation. When someone accepts Christ as his savior and gains God's forgiveness and salvation, what does he think he has received?

The most common perception is that the new Christian has been saved from the penalty of sins. "I'm a sinner. I need forgiveness. Christ died for my sins. The slate of sins against me has now been wiped clean."

He is then taught that sins committed following that cleaning of the slate can also be forgiven by a formula of repentance and confession. If he is sincere in that repentance, he will receive additional forgiveness and can restore any broken fellowship with God created by those sins. However, he can once again backslide and again lose that fellowship. There is even a debate among denominations as to whether he can even lose his salvation - for it would seem that God's tolerance would have some breaking point.

Against these inaccurate ideas, we need to consider a somewhat unusual question: Which is our greatest need? Do we need forgiveness for sins or is our greatest need righteousness? They are related to one another, but they are not the same.

Which do we need most?

Salvation is most commonly seen as the escape from the eternal penalty of sin. Christ's death brings about a covering and a forgiveness of our sin. We are sinners, but that penalty has now been paid by Christ. There is no longer an eternal penalty. This means that after this physical life is ended we will go on to an eternal life in heaven. There may still be an accounting where we will one day have to answer for the things done and said during our lifetime. But, we'll still get into heaven. The penalty of hell is not something we have to worry about any longer.

That's the common view. Salvation is an escape from the penalty of sin.

Righteousness, on the other hand, is an escape from the stain of sin. Our sin had resulted in an unrighteous state. We were unrighteous sinners. But our spiritual identity has now been changed. We are no longer even seen by God as sinners. Do we still sin? Certainly. Is God aware of our sinning? It would be ridiculous to think otherwise. But our identity in His eyes is no longer that of a sinner. We have become His righteous children and because of the work of Christ on our behalf we always live in that right standing with God. That right standing could never be accomplished or maintained by our doing. It can only come by God's grace through the justifying work of Christ.

So, which do we need the most? Forgiveness or righteousness?

It is not necessary to debate this need because true salvation actually encompasses both forgiveness and righteousness. It's as if salvation is the title of the book and there is a whole chapter on righteousness. But unfortunately we often only read some of the chapters of that book and we don't have an understanding of the full story.

Paul's Gospel

The Apostle Paul's basic gospel message is that God gives us something greater than just pardon alone. God declares us righteous. This is a main teaching of Romans chapter three: God doesn't just save us from the penalty of sin. He also grants us the gift of righteousness.

> But now apart from the law the righteousness of God has been made known, to which the Law and the Prophets testify. This righteousness is given through faith in Jesus Christ to all who believe. There is no difference between Jew and Gentile, for all have sinned and fall short of the glory of God, and all are justified freely by his grace through the redemption that came by Christ Jesus. God presented Christ as a sacrifice of atonement, through the shedding of his blood —to be received by faith. He did this to demonstrate his righteousness, because in his forbearance he had left the sins committed beforehand unpunished — he did it to demonstrate his righteousness at the present time, so as to be just and the one who justifies those who have faith in Jesus. Where, then, is boasting? It is excluded. Because of what law? The law that requires works? No, because of the law that requires faith. For we maintain that a person is justified by faith apart from the works of the law. (Romans 3:21-28)

When Paul summarizes what Christ has done for us, he refers to that work as "the righteousness from God." He teaches that we are "justified freely by his grace."

"Justified" is a legal term. It means "made righteous." When we are justified, we are not just *declared* righteous, but we are actually *made* righteous. Our sin has been placed on Christ, and then His righteousness has been granted to us (2 Corinthians 5:21). His righteousness does not just hide our sin; we are actually given the gift of His righteousness.

Notice that Paul says Christ was offered as a sacrifice of "atonement." (Romans 3:25) This New International Version mistranslation is an unfortunate reading. Atonement literally denotes a "covering of sin." The sin is still there, but it is covered so that God doesn't see it. (I'm pretty sure God has x-ray vision!)

Most English translations do not follow the New International Version's interpretation. The Greek word (*hilasterion*) sometimes rendered as "atonement" is more commonly translated "propitiation" or "expiation". These two theological words are often read hurriedly without realizing their meaning. Both words express the thought of "being removed or taken away". Their distinction with "atonement" is an important one. Our sins have not just been covered by Christ's work; they have been completely removed and taken away!

Romans 3:21-28 describes other truths about this righteousness from God.

- It is apart from the Law and it is through faith in Christ. (3:22,28)
- This righteousness is needed by all for all have sinned. (3:23)

- The righteousness from God is free and is only by His grace. (3:24)
- It is based on the sacrificial death of Christ. (3:25) Therefore it eliminates man's boasting.
- And it is all done by Christ for us. (3:27)

Let us go back now to our question. Which do we need most? Is our need salvation (as typically defined) or righteousness? What is the difference? What are the implications?

If we are only saved from sin's penalty,
then additional sin should incur more penalties.

At the moment of receiving Christ, we are forgiven of all of our sins no matter how terrible. His blood washes us white as snow. But is that moment of perfect holiness forfeited with my next sin? At least, with my next big sin?

This is the way many Christians see it. And that understanding is taught at nearly every altar call given in churches today. It is actually logical.

"Christ died for my sins. I have accepted his salvation. I am clean and pure and forgiven. I have escaped condemnation and am headed for heaven. But I continue to sin. And so I need to seek ongoing forgiveness or God will hold my sins committed since salvation against me."

I remember thinking in the years when I believed this to be the case that it would be wiser to not accept Christ until just before the moment of death. That way I would be guaranteed to stand before God in complete holiness! Of course, this is hazardous since we can't know when that moment will be.

Some who hold this view of repeated forgiveness attempt to resolve the problem while still magnifying the significance of Christ's sacrifice on the cross. They say that we will never suffer the full extent of our sins because of Christ's death on the cross, but there still will be varying levels of rewards in heaven. But others believe that additional sins can result in the loss of salvation.

If we are only saved from the penalties of sin, then it would be true that we would also need a system to deal with additional sins as they are committed. We would have to avoid further penalties incurred after our initial salvation and cleansing. But what if we don't receive a temporary or contingent forgiveness? What if we are given a righteousness not based on works but based instead on grace?

If we are given an unearned righteousness, then there is only one way that our position could be changed and our righteousness lost. God would have to change His mind. He would have to rewrite His own rules. God would have to face a contradiction of His own making. He would first see me in my unrighteous condition and He would see that I don't merit righteousness. And He would agree that I could never earn it or keep it. So He would decide by His grace to declare me righteous.

But then He would have to decide that I don't deserve to be righteous anymore because I am acting unrighteously. And He would have to take my righteousness away because I no longer deserved it. This would make God inconsistent. And it would cause the righteousness given by His grace to become dependent upon my works.

**If we are only saved, then we are still sinners —
but we are sinners saved by grace.**

You have seen the bumper sticker, "I'm just a sinner saved by grace." It is intended as a statement of humble recognition of our salvation. It is also very poor theology.

If salvation from the penalty of sin is all we have received, then it is true that we are sinners saved by grace. But if we are given God's righteousness, then we are saints in His eyes.

What difference does this make? It leads to a totally different perspective of how God sees and accepts us.

If I'm a saved sinner, I still sin and God still sees me as a sinner. I have to question God's acceptance when my goodness slips. But if I am a saint, God always sees me as holy even when I sin. I never for a moment doubt God's acceptance.

There is no verse in the Bible that refers to Christians as "sinners saved by grace." That designation is only heard in some popular Christian songs and read on bumper stickers. The Bible does however refer to believers as "saints." Sixty-three times.

**If we are only saved from sin's penalty,
then God is watching us to catch us in more sin.**

Baylor University professors Paul Froese and Christopher Bader published the results of a survey identifying the various views that American adults have of God. Their book entitled *America's Four Gods: What We Say about God-- & What that Says about Us* (Oxford University Press, 2010) revealed four different opinions of how God interacts with His world.

31.4 percent of American adults see God as an authoritative God who watches over the world in order to punish those who violate His rules. This God is very judgmental and very engaged.

23 percent view God as a benevolent God that intervenes into our world to rescue us and guide us. He is engaged, but He is not judgmental.

Others see God as a distant God that set the universe in motion but has no further involvement with it after creation. 24.4 percent of adults hold this view. Another 16 percent believe in a critical God who is not involved in our daily lives, but who will judge humans in an afterlife. This God is judgmental but not engaged. (Note: Another 5.2 percent are atheists and do not believe in a God.)

As we analyze those responses we see that almost half (47.4%) of American adults see God as a judgmental God. And another 29.6 percent see God as distant and removed or they don't believe in a God at all.

A survey that only polled Christians would possibly yield different results, but it's likely that a high percentage of Christians would also express that they view God as judgmental.

This fits nicely into a limited understanding of salvation. We need to be saved because of our sinfulness but we always remember that God is still watching for other sinful behavior. In this viewpoint, we are saved sinners who are still sinning.

But if we have been made righteous, God is no longer judging us. His decision has already been made.

And what's more, because we are totally righteous, God is now able to indwell us. Perfect righteousness is a necessary prerequisite for God's presence in our lives – and since we have actually been made holy - a holy God can now live in us.

We see this thought process confirmed in the history of Israel. The temple contained a designated most holy place where God dwelt. Elaborate procedures were in place because it was so holy. Called the "Holy of Holies", it was separated from the rest of the temple by a thick veil. Priests could enter behind that veil only on specified occasions. And they could only enter it alone. When the priest did enter, he wore a bell and a rope tied to his feet. Why? So that the worshippers remaining outside could hear the bell ringing and know that the priest was still living and had not died when encountering the holiness of God.

And why the rope? So that in the event that the priest did die, no one would have to risk their death by going in for him. He could be dragged out.

Those ancient worshippers realized that God was perfectly holy and that man was not. But when God makes us holy and righteous, *we can become His temple.* He can come and live within us. That indwelling would be brief and limited if we are pardoned and saved from sin only. But since we are righteous and holy, His Spirit's indwelling is an unchanging constant.

If we are only saved – and if we can maintain it, then there is some room for boasting.

Many Christians are fully aware of the need for Christ's salvation offered to them through His death on the cross. But after that, they are taught they are responsible to follow and obey Him in order to remain pleasing to God. They can ask God for help, but basically it is up to them. If they can live a God-pleasing life – or at least perform at a level above the curve - then they deserve to boast and become prideful. They can even look down upon or pity others.

But if righteousness is given apart from the Law and our works, then there is no room for boasting. It is the result of God's grace. Boasting is not possible because our righteousness is absolutely zero percent dependent upon us.

The Big Question

So the important question becomes, "Is a believer only saved from the penalty of his sins committed before salvation or is he perfectly righteous in God's eyes?" Those two different results have great significance in our true spiritual understanding.

We should never minimize salvation in any way, but we should desire to elevate it to its true level. The truth is that we cannot separate righteousness and salvation because righteousness is one of the several components of salvation. It is very common however to miss the implications of our righteousness. In much preaching today the important clarification is not being made.

Salvation is not just an escape from sin's penalty; it is the foundation of a relationship with a righteous and holy God. It is a relationship that God offers to us. That relationship is not based on our righteousness; it is based on the work of Christ and the righteousness of Christ that is credited to us.

When we accept that gift, then God comes and lives in us. He transforms us; He shows through us. As we abide in

Him and He abides in us, we begin to demonstrate His righteousness. It is not a righteousness of works, but a righteousness from God that comes from faith in Jesus Christ to all who believe.

That is what the Bible teaches. That is the basic truth. This is a part of the message of unfiltered grace.

CHAPTER SIX

RIGHTEOUSNESS MADE CERTAIN

It had been a long wait but I eventually heard my name called. The moment I had been dreading for what seemed to me like half an eternity had now arrived.

I walked forward with a sense of impending dread. A long while back it had been a relief to learn that they went in alphabetical order. Plus, as I had waited in my place I had figured out that they were also going by the century of one's birth. Not only was "Langley" near the middle of the alphabet, but I had just over twenty other centuries to sit through.

But all that was past. It was now my turn.

The video screen was bigger than any I had ever seen. But more than that, the resolution was so crystal sharp that the picture seemed three dimensional.

And then suddenly, I was on the big screen. I had forgotten how skinny I had been as a kid. And I was soaking wet! Oh, yeah. That was the baptismal room at the church. The video blurred as it fast-forwarded to a scene on a school playground. I listened in embarrassment at the words coming from my mouth. Then it skipped to a scene of a classroom. My mouth was closed and I wasn't speaking, but wasn't that my childhood voice? Then I realized that my unspoken thoughts were being made audible.

Over the playback of the next days, months and years I watched every impure thought, every unkind word, every wrong action of my whole life played out on that screen. And when it was finally over, the video began all over again. This time there was a split screen. On one side I saw what I had done while on the other side of the immense screen a parallel life played out and revealed all the good things that I failed to do.

I lost all track of time. But I did know this: There was a lot of video still to be played.

This nightmare scenario is likely feared by any Christian who has ever sat through a church revival sermon. We are reminded that we will give an account for every word, every action, even every thought!

All of our unworthiness will be laid bare. And everyone will know it.

With instilled scenarios like this, there is no wonder that many people have an uncertainty about where they stand with God. They try to please Him, but they never know if they are doing enough.

But some people are brutally honest. They despair because they know that they are not doing enough. The worry only increases as they hear they should doing even more. When they listen to sermons or read devotional books, they are told that they need to be more devoted and disciplined. But they still skip opportunities for prayer, Bible study, and witnessing. And they don't volunteer enough.

Some people have a real sense of guilt with little doubt about how their video will play out. They well know the reality of sin's presence in their lives. Most times they cannot even go a few hours without sinning – much less a whole day! They try to stay confessed up, but they fear they might forget something. Or, perhaps God's patience will run out and He will not hear their prayers for forgiveness any more.

Either way, they fear God's coming judgment upon their Christian lives.

Psychologists tell us that a healthy relationship cannot exist between two parties when guilt is present. There will be uncertainty and doubts. There may be resentment. There might even be an acting out with rebellion being expressed. But there cannot be a sense of full acceptance. We see this in broken marriages, dysfunctional families, and chronically low self-esteemed individuals.

And neither can we have a healthy relationship with God as long as guilt is involved. We will be uncertain of our standing. There will be feelings of failure. This might lead to resentment. And there might be actions of rebellion. Or there might just be an abandonment of our beliefs altogether.

That's why it is so crucial to understand that our guilt has been handled. The whole sin issue was resolved by the work of Christ on the cross. His sacrifice was adequate to handle all of our sin. All of it. Once and for all. And when we realize and accept that truth, then our focus can move on to the new life we have in Christ.

Many Christians don't understand this. The evidence is clear because they get hung up with the sin issue and don't understand how to move on. The focus for many is on the question, "What have I done?" Or, we can feel hopeless in our questioning, "How can I stop doing what I am doing?" This robs us of our consideration of our true need, "How can I experience the new life of Christ living in me?"

This is why it is so absolutely crucial to understand what Jesus accomplished at the cross. The penalty for sin was fully paid. The guilt issue between man and God was resolved. We were fully reconciled. Our past, present, and future sins were covered by His once for all sacrifice.

This is not just our wishful thinking. It is the consistent teaching of the New Testament.

Theological Words

Occasionally, we encounter words in our Bible reading that are not a part of our everyday language. We know they are important, but we might not fully understand their specific meaning. This is unfortunate because it causes us to have only a partial understanding of what Jesus makes possible for us.

We saw one such word, "propitiation," in chapter four. Sometimes the term is translated "expiation." It sounds theological, but what is it?

As we saw earlier, these terms signify the "removal of guilt." Not only is our sin paid for through the work of Christ, but our guilt is removed. That guilt no longer exists because there is no longer anything standing between us and God. It has not been covered; it has been taken away. Erased. Gone. That is not because of a human action created by our sorrow or penance. God did it.

Another minimally understood word is the term "sanctification." Literally, the term means "the act of being made holy." "Holy" means we are totally pure in God's eyes. And realize that God's definition of holiness does not have degrees. Something or someone cannot be mostly holy or 99% holy. It is all or none. But the Bible says that we are holy in God's sight and indwelt by His Holy Spirit. The act of sanctification is the rationale for the Apostle Paul consistently referring to Christians as "saints."

"Justification" is another theological word we encounter but might not fully understand. Justification refers to being made righteous in God's estimation. We can never justify ourselves. We can only be justified by God.

Understanding these words helps us see that God's acceptance is multi-fold. We have forgiveness, and we have righteousness. Our sin has been propitiated. We have been sanctified by God. And we have been justified. But while these terms express clear Bible teachings, we too often don't accept or we don't apply the concepts. And sometimes we add qualifiers. We might know what the Bible says, but we don't catch what it means.

As Righteous as Christ?

We all have in our minds a person that we consider to be more righteous than anyone else we know. It might be a parent or grandparent. It might be a fellow church member or a pastor. Perhaps it is a public figure like Mother Theresa, the Pope, or Billy Graham. We would never consider ourselves to be at that same level of righteousness. And it would certainly be heresy to consider that we could even approach being as righteous as Christ.

But what does God say? He says that in His eyes we are as righteous as Jesus Christ because the righteousness of Christ has been credited to us. We don't deserve that. But God says that it is true. And He doesn't just decide it and declare it – although that would certainly be enough!

He also makes it so. We are justified and sanctified because of the propitiation Christ accomplished.

Forgiven how much?

This complete and accomplished work of Christ leads to what I have found to be the part of the grace message that is most filtered in our minds and teachings.

How complete and finished is our forgiveness?

We are forgiven and made righteous when we place our trust in Christ's death on our behalf. But what happens when we sin after that? Do we lose our righteousness? Is our holiness forfeited? Is our relationship or fellowship with God affected? Don't we need to seek additional forgiveness?

CHAPTER SEVEN

FINISHED FORGIVENESS

Let's consider two fictional case studies. These examples are composites drawn from actual individuals I have met. While the stories might appear fictional, I assure you the truth of the situations is not made up.

"Church Drop-Out Joe"

"Church Drop-Out Joe" does not go to church except at Easter. He has been baptized and considers himself to be a Christian. The reason that he doesn't go to church is because he feels guilty. He has done some things for which he feels God could never forgive him. He has often confessed his sins and prayed for forgiveness, but he then committed the same sins again. He feels God probably runs out of patience with him. He hopes, hopes, hopes that he will get into heaven. He prays to God during times of extreme difficulty, but he doesn't have much confidence that God is pleased with him.

"Hope Church Will Help Me Joe"

"Hope Church Will Help Me Joe" does not stop going to church because he feels too guilty. Actually "Hope Church Will Help Me Joe" is the opposite of "Church Drop-Out Joe." He goes to church because he does feel guilty. He keeps up a front and he knows that he is not the person many people think him to be. He has thoughts and habits and responses that are wrong. He knows it. He is truly sorry, and he often asks God to forgive him. He goes to church because he needs a weekly soul cleansing.

Sometimes it carries over into most of his week. Sometimes he blows it first thing Monday morning. He prays to God often asking for forgiveness, but he doesn't have much confidence that God is pleased with him.

Both of these Joes need to hear the message of unfiltered grace. They need to hear that God is not mad at them.

How forgiven are we?

There is a clear and consistent Biblical teaching that God has made us an incredible offer. He has offered to take our sins and place them upon Jesus. And He will then take the righteousness of Jesus and place it upon us.

And He has given us forgiveness. But that's not the problem our two Joes are concerned about.

Like most Christians, they believe that they are totally, fully, completely, one hundred percent forgiven at the moment of salvation, but then they still need to receive additional incremental forgiveness to cover their sins after salvation.

Is this how forgiveness works? Is it a definite forgiveness, but only up to a certain point?

Or did salvation create a *potential* forgiveness? Does that forgiveness come into effect as long as specific additional steps are activated? Is it in any way conditional upon other actions or responses?

The actual question is "How long does my salvation forgiveness last?" Is it good only until my first sinful deed after receiving salvation? Or, does salvation bring the main forgiveness that makes future forgiveness possible?

What if I told you that you are totally, fully, completely, one hundred percent forgiven at the moment of salvation and that your forgiveness will never be lost? It does not have to be renewed. It does not have to be kept up to date.

What if I told you that if you have accepted God's redemption through Christ, your forgiveness was fully accomplished? You are forgiven.

What if I told you that your forgiveness is not conditional upon confessing and asking for additional forgiveness? Instead, it is based upon the completed work of Christ upon the cross. And since that work was adequate and final, you no longer need to seek additional forgiveness.

And what if I told you that once you have accepted Christ's sacrificial death that took away your sins, you are forgiven? It is a finished forgiveness. You no longer need to ask God for more forgiveness. There is no method or process that you do to add to or to activate what God has already done.

That belief would lead to peace and rest and joy and relief and gratefulness if you were to realize it. But that particular view is actually troublesome to most people. It is certainly not the perspective of most Christians.

In fact, I have found this single teaching to raise the most objections to the message of unfiltered grace. People will nod their heads at many truths about grace but this teaching will cause them to shake their heads at the deception they believe they are hearing.

The idea of a finished and completed forgiveness is difficult to believe. It is often met with several objections.

Objection: "That's not what I've been taught."

We have heard that Christ died for our sins and that God forgave our sins. But we have usually also heard that we should confess our sins so that God will give us an updated forgiveness.

I would say that an overwhelming majority of Christians hold this view. It is certainly the teaching of most Bible study literatures and sermons. We are urged to confess our sins daily and to keep a short account with God. Most church services conclude with an emphasis on seeking forgiveness. We are even taught that we are to include a blanket request for forgiveness near the end of our prayers: "And forgive us of our many sins."

But this prevalent belief does not have a solid foundation in scripture. It is the result of a misunderstanding of an Old Testament event and the development of a penance system in church history.

The Day of Atonement

The Day of Atonement was the most anticipated day on the Jewish calendar. It was the day that the High Priest would enter into the innermost area in the temple to intercede for the people. An unblemished lamb would be sacrificed and the blood of that lamb would be poured upon a goat.

This goat, designated as the scapegoat, would then be driven into the wilderness, thus removing and carrying away the sins of the people.

For a blessed joyful moment all the worshippers were cleansed of their sins. They were fully forgiven. But there was a major shortcoming of the idea.

57

It would not be long until another sin was committed and the personal purity was lost. That is why the Day of Atonement was always on the annual calendar.

Christians live under a New Covenant based upon a different Lamb. They hear that Christ is a superior priest that offered a superior sacrifice. They believe that Christ accomplished His work and sat down because it was fully finished. They believe it because the New Testament says it is so.

But they continue to hold onto this Old Testament concept. They are forgiven by the sacrifice and blood of Christ, but other opportunities for forgiveness have to be available.

Church History

It was only within a few hundred years following the death of Christ that the established church added the sacraments of penance and forgiveness. Sins could be absolved and forgiven through a confessional system that was overseen by the Church. A frequent participation in the sacrament was instructed by Canon Law. The code required all church members who had attained the age of discretion to confess serious sins at least once a year.

Following the Reformation of the Church in the sixteenth century, Protestants broke away from the Roman Catholic Church. Most Protestants no longer participated in the sacraments of penance, but they did continue to hold onto the idea of a need for repeated forgiveness.

Guilt

Guilt might also hold a role in the retention of a system for repeated forgiveness. As a young preacher, I discovered that much of what people judged as good preaching created guilt. I was actually once told by a congregant that I needed to "step on toes harder."

Why do people desire this brow-beating? I think it is because our consciences create guilt and we need a means to deal with that guilt. We might not see the need to confess our sins to a priest or pastor, but individual confession to God and asking Him for forgiveness relieves this guilt. It gives us a way to get rid of it.

All of these ideas create a failure to fully accept and understand what the Bible says about our holiness and righteousness. They actually reduce the full meaning of the work of Christ. And they reveal a faulty understanding of the New Covenant relationship we now have with God.

Objection: The Bible teaches we should ask God for additional forgiveness.

This is the main argument for the belief that we need to seek repeated forgiveness: "The Bible says so."

What exactly does the Bible say about a confession of sins and asking God for a repeatable forgiveness after salvation? There are three applicable passages. Jesus taught it. James spoke of it. And 1 John 1:9 is one of the most relied upon verses in the Bible for the Christian life. It tells us that God will purify us from all unrighteousness if we confess our sins.

While it is mentioned only these three times, I believe that just one Biblical teaching is sufficient to establish the truth of a matter. But what do these three passages teach?

Confess Your Sins to Others

One of the passages specifically mentioning confession of sins is found in the book of James.

> "Therefore confess your sins to each other and pray for each other so that you may be healed." (James 5:16)

James instructs us to confess our sins. But why do we confess and to whom do we make our confession?

This verse speaks of admitting our sins and being transparent with other believers. It counsels us to admit faults to fellow Christians and to request their prayers. The instructed confession is made to fellow Christians; there is no mention of confessing to God.

The Lord's Prayer

But what about Jesus' statement in the Lord's Prayer? Doesn't Jesus Himself clearly instruct us to pray and ask for the forgiveness of our sins?

> "Forgive us our sins, for we also forgive everyone who sins against us." (Luke 11:4)

Most Christians believe that this teaching is relevant and intended for today. Even the study notes in many Bibles and commentaries state that Jesus was speaking of a daily forgiveness which is necessary to restore broken communion with God.

What I am about to say will be disconcerting to some because it was not what we were taught in Sunday School and Vacation Bible School, but the truth of it is irrefutable.

When did Jesus pray this? That is, at what point in His ministry? Check it out in your Bible and identify the stage in His ministry that He gave these instructions. You will find that He taught this model of praying before His sacrificial death.

Jesus had not yet died on the cross. Salvation had not yet been accomplished. The veil separating the Holy of Holies had not yet been torn by God.

And man was still under the daily and weekly and annual sacrificial system. He did need incremental and repeated forgiveness because Jesus had not yet made the final sacrifice. He did need a way to deal with his sin.

That's the point. After Jesus died for sins once and for all, there is no longer the need to seek repeated forgiveness. No more sacrifices are required.

Jesus taught in this prayer that a man should forgive others if he wanted God to forgive him. And that was true at that *point in time*. But after the cross we are taught a different rationale for forgiving others.

> Be kind and compassionate to one another, forgiving each other, just *as in Christ God forgave you.* (Ephesians 4:32, italics added)

If the disciples had asked Jesus in one of His post-resurrection appearances to give them directions on how to pray, would He still have spoken about a conditional forgiveness? Or, would He have explained to them the once for all forgiveness He had just made possible?

If you have never considered the context of this prayer before, you might be hesitant to accept this interpretation. But if we want to understand the truth of Jesus' teachings, we do have to understand and consider context. Is the Lord's Prayer an Old Covenant or a New Covenant prayer?

Under which covenant do you choose to relate to God?

1 John 1:9 – "The Christian Soap"

"If we confess our sins, He is faithful and just and will forgive us our sins and purify us from all unrighteousness." (1 John 1:9)

This is one of the most memorized verses in our Bibles. And it creates the single biggest objection to the teaching of finished forgiveness.

John wrote this letter to Christians for he clearly mentions the readers as being children of God. But what was he writing to them about? Once again, an accurate understanding has to consider the teaching in context.

John was addressing the first major heresy of the New Testament Church. A group of men known as the Gnostics (from the Greek "*gnosis*" or "to know") was infiltrating the church with false and dangerous teachings.

The Gnostics taught that a spiritual God could not be connected nor concerned with physical matters. Therefore, there was no such thing as sin, for anything in the spiritual world could not be impacted by the physical world. Even more heretically, the Gnostics said that Jesus could not be God, for God would never join Himself with the physical.

So the Gnostics were teaching that there was no such thing as sin. This meant that no savior was needed. And Jesus was not the Son of God.

John was writing to Christians well aware of these erroneous teachings that were infiltrating the church. And he responded:

> "If we claim to be without sin, we deceive ourselves and the truth is not in us. If we confess our sins, He is faithful and just and will forgive us our sins and purify us from all unrighteousness." (1 John 1:8-9)

What was John saying? He was not talking about a required activity on the part of Christians; he was talking about the heretical teachings of the Gnostics. (Sometimes the question is raised about John speaking in the first person "we" and "ourselves", but John is not referring to himself and the recipients of his letter; he is referring to all men who have sinned and need a Savior.) John says that the Gnostics are deceiving themselves when they claim to be without sin. But if they will acknowledge their sin and confess their need for a savior, God will make them holy and righteous. Just as He does for all who come to Him for salvation.

A confirming point to consider here is the promise of a purifying from "all" unrighteousness. Is it possible to recall and confess every sin? Is righteousness lost when we sin and then regained when we confess that sin? No. Did we receive our initial forgiveness because of our confession of sin or because of the work of Christ on the cross? Can we maintain our forgiveness by confession of sin or is it by continued reliance upon the work of Christ? That is why the cross is the *only* way for the righteousness issue to be handled once and for all.

John knew that the only way to salvation was through a belief in Christ. He was not talking about a cleansing forgiveness for Christians. He was talking about a salvation prayer for those who realize their need for God's true Savior.

Later John does switch his comments to his Christian readers:

> "I write to you, dear children, because your sins *have been* forgiven on account of his name." (1 John 2:12, italics added)

Does John say that the children of God need to seek additional and supplemental forgiveness? No, that was not in fitting with his context. Christians needed to be reminded that they had been forgiven, but it was not due to a confessional ritual. They had been forgiven on account of the name and work of Jesus.

I typically encounter sincere resistance to this interpretation of 1 John 1:9. The religious filters and established beliefs are very strong. But consider this. If 1 John 1:9 *is* talking to Christians, did John know something that no other New Testament writer knew?

Paul does not teach us to pray asking for forgiveness. He doesn't instruct the Christians in Rome or Galatia or Ephesus or Philippi or Colossae or Thessalonica to do so. He doesn't tell Titus or Timothy to teach it. He never even mentions it to the church at Corinth that had really gotten off course.

Peter never encourages us to seek additional forgiveness. The writer of Hebrews never mentions this lesson.

And what about the Resurrected Lord Jesus? He never outlined a process for an updated forgiveness.

If the teaching is as crucial as it would seem to be and if it is a critical step for maintaining our fellowship with God, wouldn't some other Bible author have included a mention of it?

Or, was it never a lesson necessary to be given to children of God? Was it intended for those who had not yet received salvation?

As you consider the contextual meanings of these passages, please do not get distracted by a confusion of the value of genuine confession. While the New Covenant scriptures do not demand a confession of sins in order to receive God's forgiveness, it is important to clarify that there is a need and role for confession in the Christian life. Confession refers to an acknowledgment of our sins and a recognition of our self-reliance. We need to ask God to reveal His ways to us and we need to realize when we have gone a different way. But there is no additional forgiveness to be sought. That has already been given.

Objection: It's not about lost relationship; it's about lost fellowship.

Since the forgiveness of sin is so adequately accomplished on the cross, adherents of a "Christian soap" interpretation of 1 John 1:9 often engage in a splitting of theological hairs.

According to their understanding, our sin does not cause us to lose our "relationship" with God, but it breaks our "fellowship" with God. We need confession and forgiveness to stay in right fellowship.

This might be a clever side step, but the Bible never makes that distinction. Man makes that distinction so that our accepted ideas don't conflict with the teaching of scripture.

The Bible says that Christ gives us *eternal* fellowship with God. His death makes us holy and without fault in God's eyes.

> "He will keep you strong to the end, so that you will be blameless on the day of our Lord Jesus Christ. God, who has called you into fellowship with His Son Jesus Christ our Lord is faithful." (1 Corinthians 1:8-9)

And this idea about being blameless is written to the Corinthians no less! And God had called them into fellowship with His blameless Son.

There is no distinction made in the Bible between "relationship" with God and "fellowship" with God. They are synonyms. The *Greek* word *koinonia* means "spiritual union." Fellowship is our spiritual union and our relationship with God. He has joined us to Himself.

The term *fellowship* appears nineteen times in the New Testament. Most of the references refer to the spiritual connection that the children of God have with one another. Only a few of the references speak of a fellowship with God.

We have already seen 1 Corinthians 1:9. Here are the other references:

> "If you have any encouragement from being united with Christ, if any comfort from his love, if any fellowship with the Spirit..." (Philippians 2:1a)

"We proclaim to you what we have seen and heard, so that you also may have fellowship with us. And our fellowship is with the Father and with his Son, Jesus Christ." (1 John 1:3)

"If we claim to have fellowship with him yet walk in the darkness, we lie and do not live by the truth. But if we walk in the light, as he is in the light, we have fellowship with one another, and the blood of Jesus, his Son, purifies us from all sin." (1 John 1:6-7)

Each of these references to fellowship is about a *lasting* relationship we now have with God. We have commonly tried to differentiate between the two, but the ideas of fellowship and relationship are expressing the same spiritual union made possible by Christ. They are one and the same.

It may be a common approach to argue that Christians can damage their fellowship with God while maintaining a relationship, but the distinction between the idea of fellowship and relationship is not supported by scripture.

Objection: I just feel better when I cover all my bases.

I once had a lady tell me that she believed all that I was saying about a finished forgiveness and the unnecessary need to ask for additional forgiveness. But she continued, "I just feel better if I cover all my bases. I'm still going to pray for forgiveness."

What about her idea? Is it okay?

Andrew Farley gives a thought provoking example in his wonderful book, *The Naked Gospel*.

Let's say you are a married man. Imagine if every night before you went to sleep, you leaned over to your wife and asked her to marry you. It's just something that would make you feel better – asking her again and again. It's your way of confirming that you're married. (Andrew Farley, *The Naked Gospel*, page 147)

How would your wife respond? Would she begin to think that you didn't really understand the commitment she had made to you in her wedding vows? Would she be put at ease by your argument that it makes you *feel* better? Or, would she be concerned that you just didn't have a grasp on the reality of marriage?

Conclusion

The idea of repeatedly seeking God's forgiveness is ingrained in our religious culture, but it is not supported by scripture. We need to know that we already have God's forgiveness regardless of feelings or self-image or our desire to please God in order to earn His acceptance. Regardless of feelings of guilt, we are as holy as we will ever be. We are as righteous as we will ever be.

How can we know this is true?

We can answer some of the most common objections, but that alone is not conclusive. So, how can we know this is true?

Because it is what the Bible consistently teaches.

CHAPTER EIGHT

COMPLETED RIGHTEOUSNESS

Past teachings and legalistic religions support the idea that even though one has accepted God's forgiveness through Christ's death on the cross, it is still necessary to continue to confess one's sin in order to maintain righteousness in God's eyes.

The Bible does not support that idea. In fact, the Bible consistently underscores the finished work of Christ.

The Clear Bible Teaching about
Righteousness in Christ

There is a universal trait that every man, woman and child shares. That common bond is that we all sin at least one time in our lives. Actually, we all exceed that quota!

The commission of that sin means that we cannot be completely righteous. Just one single sin, and complete righteousness is lost. We can do righteous things half the time; we can maybe do righteous things most of the time. But that doesn't change the fact that we are unrighteous. Just one sin – even a small one – and we are unrighteous.

We might compare our righteousness to that of others. That approach might help our feelings, but it changes nothing. We might even claim to be righteous because we think we are doing all the right things and none of the wrong things. But that claim puts us at odds with the teaching of the Bible. The Bible is inarguably clear when it says,

"There is no one righteous, not even one." (Romans 3:10)

This universal and undeniable fact presents a major problem because a perfect God requires righteousness. If He is to indwell us and if we are to live in His presence, we must be holy and righteous. And we cannot just *act* holy and righteous, we must *be* holy and righteous. That true and actual righteousness can only be achieved in two ways. We stubbornly try the first, but we absolutely need the second.

We could achieve a status of righteousness by earning it. The label of righteousness would be deserved if we were to think and act and be righteous all of the time. But it doesn't sound like a hopeful analysis when the Bible declares that our human righteousness is like filthy rags in God's estimation (Isaiah 64:6). Even our best attempts fall well short of the standard.

The Bible is therefore clear that righteousness can never be earned. But there is one other way to get there. We could have our righteousness given to us by someone with the authority to do so.

God is the judge of righteousness. And He is the only judge. So what did God do?

"But now He has reconciled you by Christ's physical body through death to present you holy in His sight, without blemish and free from accusation." (Colossians 1:22)

"God made him who had no sin to be sin for us, so that in him we might become the righteousness of God." (2 Corinthians 5:21)

Christ paid the penalty for our sin so that we might receive His righteousness. And God has reconciled us to Himself declaring us holy and without blemish. That is *true* righteousness! And if God the Judge says that we possess His righteousness, then we do. The only One that counts says that it is so.

If God has made us righteous and if God has declared us righteous, what purpose do we have to continue to seek His forgiveness for our unrighteousness?

Imagine if a person of great means were to give you a million dollars. Would you leave it on the table and say, "Please give me one thousand dollars." And then the generous donor responds, "Here, I am giving you a million dollars." Would you still reply, "But would you give me one thousand dollars?"

When we continue to ask God to cleanse us from unrighteousness, it indicates that we don't understand what He has already given us. It reveals that we don't accept that He has given us a righteousness in Christ.

The Clear Bible Teaching about God's Total Forgiveness through Christ's Sacrifice

If the Bible says that our righteousness is based on the sacrifice of Christ, then what does it say is the basis for the forgiveness of our sins? It is every bit as clear and definite here.

"He forgave us all our sins, having canceled the written
code, with its regulations, that was against us and that stood
opposed to us; He took it away, nailing it to the cross."
(Colossians 2:13-14)

All of our sins. Canceled. Taken away. And when did
this forgiveness happen? Is it based upon the single event
sacrifice of Christ's death or is it incremental? Is it necessary
that forgiveness be repeated? Does our forgiveness occur one
major time and then again each time we confess and request
it again? No. The Bible reveals the completeness of our
forgiveness:

"For Christ died for sins once for all, the righteous for the
unrighteous, to bring you to God." (1 Peter 3:18)

The Bible says "once for all." Does that allow for
forgiveness to be re-enacted and reapplied in some way or
was it truly once for all? To answer the question, let us go
back to the premise of the Old Testament sacrificial system.

There were certain prescribed sacrifices for sin under
that system. Some sacrifices were to be offered throughout
the year; one main sacrifice occurred on the annual Day of
Atonement. The blood of a lamb was poured out and prayers
for forgiveness were offered. This important sacrifice was
repeated annually by the priests on behalf of the people.

Are we still under this old system or has God provided
another way? The New Testament answers this question
definitively when it teaches that we are now under a different
priestly and sacrificial system because Jesus came to be both
the priest and the sacrifice.

"Unlike the other high priests, he does not need to offer sacrifices *day after day*, first for his own sins, and then for the sins of the people. He sacrificed for their sins *once for all* when he offered himself." (Hebrews 7:27, italics added)

"When this priest had offered for all time one sacrifice for sins, he sat down at the right hand of God." (Hebrews 10:12)

Do these Bible verses indicate that we are still under a repeated sacrificial system? Does the Bible teach the concept of doing penance for specific sins? Does the Bible teach the need for repeated doses of forgiveness? Or does the Bible teach that Christ died one time for all sins and we are to put our confidence and hope in that?

Does the Bible teach a finished forgiveness?

We have seen many clear Biblical teachings about our righteousness in Christ and God's forgiveness of our sin through Christ's sacrifice. The commonly held belief that we maintain our forgiveness by repeatedly seeking forgiveness stands against those teachings.

The more that one reads the Bible in context and the more one sees the logical and non-contradictory dealing by God with our sin, the more one understands that the idea of total and complete forgiveness being given to us at salvation is the only viewpoint that fits.

Proponents of an unfiltered grace message are often accused of not believing what the Bible teaches about the idea of forgiveness. Actually the concept of a fully accomplished and complete forgiveness is the only understanding that fully takes the Bible in context.

Why is this a big deal?

What does it hurt to keep asking God for forgiveness? Why is it significant to see that our righteousness is not gained, lost, and then gained again? Why does it matter if I want to manage my sin and guilt by seeking God's forgiveness?

It is significant because Christ's gift of righteousness is minimized when we keep the focus on sin and our personal maintenance of righteousness. We are implying that God's way was not complete and thorough enough.

Continuing to ask for forgiveness indicates that we don't trust or understand that we are already forgiven. And it actually waters down the cross because it doesn't recognize the wondrous work of salvation and forgiveness.

Continuing to ask God to cleanse us of our unrighteousness indicates we don't understand that we have already received the righteousness of Christ and that we are standing not in our righteousness but we are standing in His.

But would it not be wise to go ahead and put eggs in both baskets? No, that approach contains a problematic flaw because it means one is not truly trusting in Christ's forgiveness. He is saying that the work of Christ alone is not adequate.

But if we want to cover all the bases, then maybe we should also believe in the teachings of Mohammed. And to be safe, maybe we should also burn some incense to Buddha. A Christian should find these ideas appalling. We don't need to trust in Mohammed or Buddha. The death of Christ is completely sufficient.

Exactly.

Don't keep asking or working for
something you already have.

Most Christians see no problem at all when they hear someone pray, "God, forgive us of our many sins."

But how would you feel if you heard me praying, "God, I pray you will help me find the woman you have for me to marry." Good prayer, right? But what if you knew that I've been very happily married for over thirty-five years?

Or maybe I should keep praying, "God, please give me a son. And a grandson. And a granddaughter. Please God. Bless me with grandchildren."

What would you then think when I introduced you to my son, Josh? He is now thirty-three. And my grandson Jack is five. My granddaughter Reese is two.

And what if you heard me asking God to forgive me of my many sins? And then I tell you that I believe that Jesus paid for my sins on the cross?

Would you say, "Keep asking"? Or would you wonder why I was praying for something that I already had?

CHAPTER NINE

THE BROKEN COVENANT

The idea of a finished forgiveness is a difficult truth for many to accept. Not only does it seem illogical, but it conflicts with some of our entrenched beliefs. This is the reason that the idea of completed forgiveness is one of the major sticking points with believing a message of unfiltered grace. Many Christians believe it to be a false and even misleading concept.

They will meet it with criticism and resistance because they look back upon the cross and view that sacrifice as the work of Christ that brought us salvation and forgiveness. And that's true. Jesus' death did secure our victory over sin's eternal penalty. But what about sins that are committed after salvation? It would seem logical that further sins would need additional forgiveness – thus additional confession. This is reasonable because we often tend to separate the forgiveness of sins committed prior to salvation from those committed after salvation.

A more complete understanding of the importance of the cross occurs when we see the cross not from our perspective but from God's view. What exactly did Jesus accomplish when He died on that cross?

The Dividing Line of Human History

Visit a museum and view the dated artifacts. Your visit will reveal something about the viewpoint of history. You will see that according to the world's perspective, the birth of Christ is the dividing point of history. You might never hear that stated in a museum or a history book, but note the manner in which history is dated. The universal system for dating historical events utilizes a system based on the birth of Christ. Our division of time eras is marked B.C. and A.D. ("Before Christ" and "Anno Domini" – "the year of the Lord") As world societies attempt to be more secular and more inclusive of non-Christian cultures, "Before Christ" is now being called BCE - "Before Common Era". But the point remains no matter what words are utilized: Our calendar recognizes the birth of Christ as the division point in history.

God does not view human history with that perspective. The birth of Christ might be the dividing point of world history, but it is not the dividing point in spiritual or Christian history. It doesn't mark God's key transition. God's dividing line is Christ's death on the cross. That is God's transition point. The death of Christ ended the first chapters of spiritual history and began the final chapters. In God's view, Christ's crucifixion was the transition from an old way to a new way. It marked the end of an old ineffective covenant and the implementation of a new and better covenant.

For much of my Christian life I had heard of the New Covenant. I even knew some of the details. But it was an unfiltered realization of its truth that dramatically changed my perspective of Christian living.

God's Covenant with Abraham

Believers of the One True God have a very high regard for Abraham. He was God's choice to be the Father of Israel – God's chosen people. The Apostle Paul recognized his centrality to our understanding of faith. And he was one of the key players in this idea of a New Covenant.

God told Abraham in Genesis 17:7 that he would make an everlasting covenant with his descendants.

> I will establish my covenant as an everlasting covenant between me and you and your descendants after you for the generations to come, to be your God and the God of your descendants after you.

When God declares that something is everlasting, He does not mean that it will be temporary or interim. He does not mean that it will be replaced. He means that it will last for the whole of human history.

This everlasting promise both preceded and superseded the later covenant for righteousness that would be based upon the Law. In fact it was given over four centuries before the Law was given to Moses. And this promise was given because of God's grace.

Paul spells this out clearly in Galatians 3:17-18.

> "The law, introduced 430 years later, does not set aside the covenant previously established by God and thus do away with the promise. For if the inheritance depends on the law, then it no longer depends on a promise; but God in his grace gave it to Abraham through a promise." (Galatians 3:17-18)

God's Covenant of The Law

It was then 430 years after His promise to Abraham that God made a covenant with Israel based on their full obedience. God specified clearly the people's responsibility in the keeping of that covenant.

> "Now if you obey me fully and keep my covenant, then out of all nations you will be my treasured possession." (Exodus 19:5)

The people responded unanimously to God's conditional if/then requirement. They promised, "We will keep it all."

> When Moses went and told the people all the LORD's words and laws, they responded with one voice, "Everything the LORD has said we will do." Moses then wrote down everything the LORD had said. (Exodus 24:3-4a)

And Moses made sure that the people understood what they had promised by announcing it again. He received the same response.

> Then he took the Book of the Covenant and read it to the people. They responded, "We will do everything the LORD has said; we will obey." (Exodus 24:7)

God wanted to eliminate completely any possible misunderstanding of what He was requiring. He invited Moses to meet Him on the mountain top so that Moses might receive a copy of the covenant etched in stone.

> The LORD said to Moses, "Come up to me on the mountain and stay here, and I will give you the tablets of stone, with

the law and commands I have written for their instruction."
(Exodus 24:12)

Then Moses entered the cloud as he went on up the
mountain. And he stayed on the mountain forty days and
forty nights. (Exodus 24:18)

It is very insightful what happened next. The problem
with Law as a way to righteousness was revealed before the
stone tablets were even completed and presented to Moses.

When the people saw that Moses was so long in coming
down from the mountain, they gathered around Aaron and
said, "Come, make us gods who will go before us. As for this
fellow Moses who brought us up out of Egypt, we don't
know what has happened to him." Aaron answered them,
"Take off the gold earrings that your wives, your sons and
your daughters are wearing, and bring them to me." So all
the people took off their earrings and brought them to
Aaron. He took what they handed him and made it into an
idol cast in the shape of a calf, fashioning it with a tool.
Then they said, "These are your gods, O Israel, who brought
you up out of Egypt." (Exodus 32:1-4)

Moses had been given God's Laws. Moses had faithfully
shared the Lord's words and Laws with the people. And God
then called Moses back to the top of the mountain to get the
tablets of stone that the people had unanimously pledged to
obey. But, how long did they obey? They broke their pledge
and their part of the covenant even before Moses had come
back down from the mountain!

The people were unable from the very beginning to keep this covenant that was based upon the Law. But Moses was faithful to God's words and he continued to remind the people that full obedience to this Law was their way to righteousness.

> "The Lord commanded us to obey all these decrees and to fear the Lord our God, so that we might always prosper and be kept alive, as is the case today. And if we are careful to obey all this law before the Lord our God, as he has commanded us; *that will be our righteousness.*"
> (Deuteronomy 6:24-25, italics added)

It was clear. Under this Covenant it was a careful and full obedience to all the Law that resulted in righteousness.

The Bad News

Not only did the first recipients of the Law fall short from the outset, they would continue to demonstrate that they could not do it. Each and every one sinned and fell short of God's standards.

They could keep part of the Law's commands some of the time. But *part of it* and *some of the time* were not God's specifications. He said *all of it* and *all of the time*. Jesus would later hold this standard up to the teachers and followers of the Law by reminding them that they were to be perfect as God Himself was perfect. Anything less fell short.

A reading of the Old Testament recounts the persistent pattern of disobedience, suffering, remorse, rededication and another round beginning with disobedience. But then God said that He was putting into effect a New Covenant. It had become evident that the people could not continue in the covenant based on Law, so God enacted a different contract.

> But when God found fault with the people, he said: "The day is coming," says the Lord, "when I will make a new covenant with the people of Israel and Judah. This covenant will not be like the one I made with their ancestors when I took them by the hand and led them out of the land of Egypt. They did not remain faithful to my covenant, so I turned my back on them", says the Lord. (Hebrews 8:8-9, NLT)

Why did God take this step? Had He intended that His first plan would work but was forced to admit that it was a dismal failure? Or, was this Law Covenant another step in His unfolding plan for a salvation by grace? Was a New Covenant His plan all along?

Of course it was. And when the time was right, He enacted His actual plan.

> But when the time had fully come, God sent his Son, born of a woman, born under law, to redeem those under law, that we might receive the full rights of sons. (Galatians 4:4-5)

And the ineffectiveness of the Covenant of Law revealed that God had always had a different plan for man to receive righteousness. The Old Covenant of Law paved the way and pointed toward a new righteousness that would be made possible by the sacrificial death of a redeeming Savior.

But now a righteousness from God, apart from law, has
been made known, to which the Law and the Prophets
testify. (Romans 3:21)

God would offer a New Covenant. That had been the
plan all along.

CHAPTER TEN

A NEW SYSTEM FOR RIGHTEOUSNESS

God entered into an everlasting covenant with Abraham that was not based upon the Law, but upon God's promise. Next God contracted with the people through another covenant. This covenant was explicitly based upon the peoples' obedience to the Law.

By the time of Christ's birth and life, people who worshipped God related to Him through a covenant that had been in place for almost fifteen hundred years. But God was about to initiate a New Covenant. This covenant would be based upon the sacrificial death of Christ.

An Important Detail

Most readers probably skim over the genealogies in the Gospel accounts of Matthew and Luke. It usually seems that they are just a large number of "begats" surrounded by unpronounceable names.

But there is a seemingly insignificant mention in Matthew's genealogy that is actually quite important. Matthew 1:1-2 informs us that Jesus was a descendent of Abraham, Isaac, Jacob, and Judah. Tracing Jesus' lineage back to Abraham, Isaac and Jacob certainly has some significance. But what about Judah? That doesn't seem to be that big of a deal.

The writer of Hebrews reveals why this genealogy is a noteworthy connection.

"For it is clear that our Lord descended from Judah, and in regard to that tribe Moses said nothing about priests." (Hebrews 7:14-16)

Under the Old Covenant of Law all the priests were from the tribe of Levi. This was non-negotiable. No descendant of any other tribe could be a priest. No matter how godly or how committed or how knowledgeable or how loving or how competent, they could never be a priest. They didn't meet this key qualification.

But Jesus was not from the tribe of Levi. He was from the tribe of Judah. He was not qualified to be a priest. But He was not intended to be a priest under the Old Covenant. The New Covenant was not the same as the old. A new covenant required a new priest.

It was a different system. It was based on a different sacrifice. It led to a different result. And it required a different type of priest.

First he said, "Sacrifices and offerings, burnt offerings and sin offerings you did not desire, nor were you pleased with them" (although the law required them to be made). Then he said, "Here I am, I have come to do your will." He sets aside the first to establish the second. And by that will, we have been made holy through the sacrifice of the body of Jesus Christ once for all. (Hebrews 10:8-10)

God replaced the ineffectual Covenant of Law with a New Covenant. And here is where it becomes so revolutionary for us. This New Covenant and its promises were not conditional upon the peoples' fulfillment. That had already been tried. That is why God made a new agreement. And this covenant would be radically different. This new agreement was between God and Jesus.

Jesus was not only the sacrifice for sins. His death was even more than that. He upheld and fulfilled His end of the New Covenant. He finished it.

> "The former regulation is set aside because it was weak and useless (for the law made nothing perfect), and a better hope is introduced, by which we draw near to God... Jesus has become the guarantee of a better covenant." (Hebrews 7:18-19,22)

A better hope and a new way for man to relate to God were introduced. This would not be a contract between God and man. It would be a covenant between God and Christ. Jesus would guarantee its success.

This is a rather immense idea that many Christians have never understood. I personally went decades of my Christian life before I began to see its truth and significance. I never grasped that the Book of Hebrews and many of Paul's teachings state that the New Covenant is not between God and us, but rather it is between God and Christ. I never understood the significance of the Bible teaching that in the New Covenant, the new agreement, God bypassed the people and enacted a New Covenant with a new High Priest, who lives forever to intercede and represent the people.

The Conclusion:
God entered a covenant with Jesus Christ.

God knew from the beginning (and we also learn from the example of Israel) that if He entered a covenant with man it could never last. We would never keep our end of the agreement. So instead He swore by Himself. He made an oath with Himself and He fulfilled it Himself. The Father made a covenant with the Son, appointing Him an eternal priest over the people.

> "He became a priest with an oath when God said to him,
> 'The Lord has sworn and will not change His mind, You are a
> priest forever.' Because of this oath, Jesus has become the
> guarantee of a better covenant." (Hebrews 7:21-22)

Paul saw this truth and he recognized the difference. He knew that the everlasting promises to Abraham were actually promises to Abraham's seed. For centuries, Jews had believed that they were the seeds of Abraham to whom the promises were given. But Paul taught that the people were not the "seed" mentioned in the promises God gave to Abraham. It was not referring to the Jews and it was not referring to Christians who consider themselves as the spiritual descendants of Abraham. Jesus was the Seed to whom the promises referred.

> The promises were spoken to Abraham and to his seed. The
> Scripture does not say "and to seeds," meaning many
> people, but "and to your seed," meaning one person, who is
> Christ. (Galatians 3:16)

When God made His promise to Abraham to establish an everlasting covenant, He was referring not to us humans, but to Jesus. The promise through Abraham is a promise to Jesus. This is the everlasting covenant that Jesus in the fullness of time fulfilled. The Father made a covenant with the

87

Son to represent us for the sake of righteousness. He is our intercessor. He is our righteousness.

The new superior covenant is a covenant between God and Jesus Christ. And both God and Christ faithfully keep up both ends of the agreement.

What Does This Mean?

An understanding of God's New Covenant does not just draw a slight semantic distinction. It changes everything! It means that God's opinion of Jesus as our representative isn't dependent on what we do. We are not in a covenant with God that we must uphold and maintain. Instead we are - by the inheritance of adoption - heirs to the covenant made with Christ.

If we are an heir of Christ, our righteousness in God's eyes can only fail when God's covenant with Christ fails. When our faith is in Him, nothing we do can take away His representation and the finished forgiveness He offered on our behalf.

Because this covenant is effective and enduring, God's opinion of us will never change. It's not about us. We are only the heirs of the completed work of Christ.

The old covenant – between God and man – was based on man's success in obeying all the laws, decrees and stipulations. But now our sin can only be held against us if Jesus fails to uphold His end of the agreement and His priesthood on our behalf.

Putting It All Together

God made an Old Covenant with man instituted through Moses and The Law. It was a Sin Model Covenant that didn't work out because men and women could not keep their end of it. The old agreement didn't work out for us because we couldn't live up to it.

So God entered into a New Covenant with Jesus Christ. He had known from the beginning that if He entered a covenant with us it could never last. He knew man would never keep his end of the agreement. So, the Father made a covenant with the Son, appointing Him an eternal priest over the people.

In Christ, we relate to God through a New Covenant which is a far better covenant. It is a covenant based upon the work of Christ. It is not based on what we could strive to do, but it is based upon what Christ would do. And did do.

If you are in Christ, your covenant will last as long as the Father and Christ remain faithful to their own agreement. And God has sworn. He said He will never change His mind.

Now This Starts To Make Sense

There are three occurrences associated with the story of the cross that are well-known and recognized as significant. But they are more than just accompanying events. They are central to the understanding of the New Covenant.

Last Supper

Jesus knew that the time had arrived. Fully aware of His impending arrest and death, He instructed His disciples to prepare a meal and a place so that they might share one last Passover meal together.

So on that Thursday night just hours before His arrest, He reclined at the table with them. There was a familiar script that all Hebrew men had heard their fathers and grandfathers recite. But as Jesus spoke, He added to that script. As Jesus passed that cup of wine, He said that it referred to His coming death. He revealed that His blood would make possible a New Covenant relationship with God.

> "This is my blood of the covenant, which is poured out for many for the forgiveness of sins." (Matthew 26:28)

I'm certain that the disciples must have looked at one another wondering what Jesus was saying. These were not the familiar words. This was not part of the Old Covenant they had known all their lives. And they were correct. It was about a New Covenant.

The Final Three Spoken Words

Different witnesses heard different things as they witnessed Christ's death upon the cross. The New Testament gospel writers record seven phrases that Jesus uttered.

And we also read that John was the one disciple to stand at the foot of the cross for the duration of the crucifixion. This eyewitness and writer of the fourth gospel records that Christ's final words were a short, three word sentence, "It is finished." What did Jesus mean?

Some people say that Jesus was referring to the suffering of the crucifixion. He meant that His pain was now over. Others believe that it refers to His sacrifice and payment for sin. It was now done. The price had been paid. But either of those - or both of those – misses the bigger picture. The meaning of those three words refers to Christ's covenant with God. He had fulfilled His end of the agreement.

Jesus came to be the mediator and the High Priest and the blood sacrifice of a New Covenant. But His death did not begin it. His death sealed it. The covenant would be based upon His fulfillment of God's plan. And He accomplished it. What had to happen happened. He completed it. He finished it. It was done.

The Temple Curtain Completely Torn

If we had been there at the crucifixion we would have seen Jesus suffer. We would have heard Jesus utter several phrases. We would have seen His head drop to His chest as He died. We would have heard the grief-filled cries of His mother and of those few followers who stood at the base of the cross. But at the exact moment of His death – an accompanying event of huge importance occurred. We would not have seen it, for it took place not there on that hillside, but in the temple.

In the center area of the temple in Jerusalem, there was an innermost room. It measured 30' x 30' x 30' – a perfect cube. This area was called "The Holy of Holies" and it was recognized as the actual earthly dwelling place of God's presence. This holy room could be entered only once a year on the Day of Atonement and it could only be entered by the High Priest.

The Holy of Holies did not have an entrance door. It was entered by passing through a heavy curtain. This heavy curtain or veil hung undisturbed for all but one day of the year. No one could step past that barrier which separated God's presence from the people. They could not come into God's holy presence. They were not worthy. They were not holy.

But at the precise moment of Christ's death, this heavy curtain separating man from God was torn in two. It was torn from the top to the bottom signifying that it was not torn by the hands of man, but by the power of God. It was torn in two because Christ opened the way to God.

Why is this so significant? What did it mean? It meant that a new way, a New Covenant opened our way to God. Jesus' death fulfilled and accomplished the required terms. He had fully satisfied the conditions of the New Covenant.

And all who trust in Him are made heirs of His covenant. It's not about what we might do; it is about what He did. And we are the recipients. We now have a new system for relating to God. We now have a new and different way to righteousness.

CHAPTER ELEVEN

A SUPERIOR WAY

The Book of Hebrews is one of the least studied books of the Bible. Its authorship is undetermined and the writing style is complex and often seems repetitive. Hebrews is perhaps best known for the statements about entertaining angels (13:2), the impossibility of someone falling away to be brought back to repentance (6:6), the mention of a priest named Melchizedek (6:20) and the roll call of faith in chapter 11. Much of the rest of the book is seldom quoted and many readers find it difficult to understand.

Although it might not be the most frequently studied, Hebrews is perhaps the most important book in Scripture for understanding the truth of the New Covenant. It tells us the what, the why and the how. The two Greek words for "better" and "superior" are frequently used in the letter. The overall conclusion is that the New Covenant of Grace is superior and better than the Old Covenant of Law.

In order to understand the book, one has to follow several complex arguments.

The New Covenant
Has A Superior Priest

Christ is the sinless priest of the New Covenant. As we have seen earlier, His lineage, tracing back to Judah, disqualified Him from being a priest under the guidelines of the Old Covenant. But He is the one and only priest of the New Covenant.

Not only is He sinless and perfect, but He doesn't die as all the priests from the tribe of Levi do. He does not have to be replaced by a succeeding priest. He is the superior priest who serves continually and eternally.

The New Covenant
Has A Superior Sacrifice

The Old Testament priests served in the temple offering sacrifices for the sins of the people. And they offered them repeatedly because the specified sacrifices could only cover sins. They could never take the sins away. Since sin was a continual action, the sacrifices for sins had to be continually repeated.

But Jesus the priest of the New Covenant offered a sacrifice that was so superior it would never again need to be offered. The forgiveness attained by His sacrifice was final and once for all. This reality is basic to our understanding of a finished forgiveness.

> Day after day every priest stands and performs his religious duties; again and again he offers the same sacrifices, which can never take away sins. But when this priest had offered for all time one sacrifice for sins, he sat down at the right hand of God. Since that time he waits for his enemies to be made his footstool, because by one sacrifice he has made perfect forever those who are being made holy. (Hebrews 10:11-14)

I doubt that any Christian questions whether Jesus is a superior priest. And the point about Jesus being the superior sacrifice for our sins is never questioned. Yet as we have seen earlier, the finality of that sacrifice is often not fully understood and consistently applied. But it is the third argument of Hebrews that is often overlooked by many Christians who have read and studied their Bibles.

The New Covenant Is Based On A Better Promise

The Covenant of Law was based on a promise: Obey God fully and that would be the peoples' righteousness. The New Covenant was also based on a promise.

> "But the ministry Jesus has received is as superior to theirs as the covenant of which he is a mediator is superior to the old one, and it is founded on better promises." (Hebrews 8:6)

> "The former regulation is set aside because it was weak and useless (for the law made nothing perfect), and a better hope is introduced, by which we draw near to God." (Hebrews 7:18-19)

What is this better hope to which the writer of Hebrews is referring? And what are these better promises?

The book of Hebrews further details the concept mentioned in the previous chapter of this book. It teaches that the New Covenant is not between God and man, but rather it is *between God and Christ*. In the New Covenant, God bypassed the people and entered into a New Covenant with a new High Priest. In Christ, God accepted the responsibility to uphold the covenant Himself. He takes the burden off of the shoulders of those who could never uphold it and sets them free from their bondage of debt to the Law. Christ fulfills all the terms and conditions of this New Covenant. And we become heirs of His righteousness.

The New System Doesn't Depend Upon Me

The New Covenant contained the one essential variance with the other covenants of the Bible. Time and time again man failed to uphold his side of the covenant agreements with God. God was *always* faithful to keep His side of the covenant, but man never kept his side. This was true of all of the conditional covenants.

The covenant given to Noah that God would never again destroy the earth by flood has been kept. It was unconditional. The covenant given to Abraham that his seed would be a blessing to all men was kept. It was also unconditional.

But any time man entered into a conditional equation, there was a failure to uphold that covenant. This was the reason for the failure of the Old Covenant of Law.

"For if there had been nothing wrong with that first
covenant, no place would have been sought for another. But
God found fault with the people." (Hebrews 8:7-8)

God found fault with the people. The Law itself was not the problem. The problem was not the standard. The problem was man. The Jews tried to keep the standard, but they could not. They repented and tried again. But they still could not. And so the cycle continues to repeat.

We as Christians are no more successful. We too can try to keep the standards, but we will find that we cannot. We can promise to do better, but we continue to fall short. We continue to do the very things we don't want to do while failing to do the very things we do want to do.

Why is this? It is because all efforts at controlling our own righteousness places us under a curse.

> "All who rely on observing the law are under a curse, for it is written: 'Cursed is everyone who does not continue to do everything written in the Book of the Law.' Clearly no one is justified before God by the law." (Galatians 3:10-11)

The clarity of these verses is indicting. The standard of acceptability means that we must do *everything.* That absolute standard means complete perfection and that there is no room for error. Not only must the followers of the covenant do everything, but they must *continue* to do everything. There are no limitations on the demand for perfection.

This unattainable perfection means that any attempters are under a curse. And so Paul concludes that clearly no one can be justified before God through the Law. That was the problem with the previous covenant that led God to make a New Covenant.

> "The time is coming, declares the Lord, when I will make a new covenant... It will not be like the old covenant I made with their forefathers when I took them by the hand to lead them out of Egypt, *because they did not remain faithful* to my covenant." (Hebrews 8:7-9, italics added)

The New Covenant could not be like the old one. Man could not remain faithful to that earlier one, so a different covenant was required. And it would be far better. God's New Covenant doesn't depend upon us to keep it. We don't fulfill it. Rather, Christ fulfills it for us. And we are the heirs of the covenant that He fulfilled with God.

The New System Is Possible To Keep

It is possible to keep the new system because it has already been kept! The covenant has been fulfilled because it is not based on us. It is based upon a superior sacrifice by a superior priest. By faith we become the heirs of what Jesus has done for us.

> "By one sacrifice He has made perfect forever those who are being made holy." (Hebrews 10:14)

God said, "Here, let me do it for you." And He did it.
The Old could never make men perfect. It needed repeating. And the Old could not take away sin. It only covered it. But the New is a completed work. The New doesn't cover sin, it takes it away.

The Old said, "Be perfect. Be holy." The New says, "I have made you perfect. I have made you holy. For you are heirs of the perfection and holiness and righteousness of Christ."

The New System Is Not "Out There" But "In Here"

The requirements of the Old Covenant were inscribed onto tablets of stone. They were later copied onto scrolled parchments which could be touched and handled. They could be read and they could be heard. They could be memorized. They could be displayed. But the laws of the New Covenant were not to be written on tablets of stone. God would write them on men's hearts.

> "This is the covenant I will make with them after that time, says the Lord. I will put my laws in their hearts, and I will write them on their minds." (Hebrews 10:16)

The plurality of the word "laws" is significant. Whenever the Bible refers to the body of Law – the Old Covenant standard for righteousness – it is singular. It is usually preceded by the article "the." In our English translations, it is often capitalized.

But this reference in Hebrews 10:16 is not to "The Law", but to God's laws. God's New Covenant laws are not referring to a standard of righteousness for us to attain, but a way of life that is being lived out in us as we are transformed and led by the Spirit of God.

The Law is always a list. And the list always keeps growing. We are to learn the list and follow the list and teach the list. But God's laws are written on our hearts and on our minds. They actually come from the Spirit of Christ living in our lives. They are the fruit of the Spirit. God's laws are the life of Christ showing through our lives.

Then and Now

Meet Joseph. Joseph is a Jewish man and a member of God's chosen people. He eagerly looked for a coming Messiah but he lived and died long before the coming of Christ. Joseph was fervent about his obedience to God's Law and he faithfully participated in the offering of sacrifices for his sin and for the sins of his family. Joseph would never hear of a better way and a better system.

Now meet Joe. Joe is a Christian living today. Joe loves God and has accepted Jesus as his Savior. Joe has heard that God has included him in a new and better system. But what does Joe do? He continues to take up parts of the old system.

Joe believes that he is responsible for fulfilling God's Law. He thinks that righteousness is earned or at least that it is lessened by our sins. He believes that God's forgiveness needs repeating. Joe would laugh at the idea of sacrificing goats or bulls, but he does feel he should make other payments. And he does feel the need to repeat the confessional formulas for forgiveness.

Joseph and Joe are living in very similar spiritual worlds. But has anything dramatically changed in the time between their generations?

Obviously. The promised Christ did come and He did die as the final sacrifice for sin. And almost all Christians would raise their hands if someone were to ask, "How many of you believe Jesus said at the time of his death, 'It is finished'?"

And what would be the response if they were asked, "How many of you believe Jesus meant it when He said that it was finished?" Again, almost all would raise hands.

But what if they were then asked, "How many of you feel we still need to ask God for additional forgiveness?" I think the response would be the same. Almost all would raise hands.

It seems that it is common to miss the truth that we are now relating to God under a new system. And even when we read or hear about the differences between the two covenants, the tendency and history of the two systems is that man wants to combine them.

But Jesus said that you can't do that. He said that you can't mix the two.

> He told them this parable: "No one tears a patch from a new garment and sews it on an old one. If he does, he will have torn the new garment, and the patch from the new will not match the old. And no one pours new wine into old wineskins. If he does, the new wine will burst the skins, the wine will run out and the wineskins will be ruined. No, new wine must be poured into new wineskins. (Luke 5:36-38)

Jesus declared that the old and the new could not be mixed. He used the analogies of new cloth being sewed onto old fabric or new wine being poured into old wineskins. But His point was about the New Covenant He was bringing into effect. Not only would it be replacing the old, it would not be able to be combined with the old. The two were too different.

It's Our Choice

We each decide which system we want to live by. Do we want to try to fulfill the first system? Then simply keep the Law perfectly and we will make it. No one other than Jesus has done it so far, but do we want to try it as our way to righteousness?

We also each decide which system we want to be judged by. Do we want to be judged by how well we do and act and think and work? Or do we want to trust and accept and be an heir of the righteousness of Christ?

But we can't try both. They actually negate each other because they are mutually exclusive.

The old approach failed because it was dependent upon man's willpower and commitment. This new approach draws upon God's divine power. And that power provides us with everything we truly need for life and godliness.

The Sad Reality

Many Christians still relate to God by this Old Covenant based on law and obedience. Their focus on sin management causes them to miss the wonderful blessing of the New Covenant. They still believe that they are the creators of their own righteousness.

But right standing with God is not based on our keeping a covenant. It is based on the work of Christ and His fulfillment of a New Covenant. He did it. We cannot do it and we cannot undo it. Pleasing God and staying in right standing with Him is not based upon our keeping a covenant.

And this New Covenant is not a weak and unstable covenant that we occasionally fall out of, forcing us to reestablish our covenant relationship over and over again. There is no need to ask for forgiveness again and again. The Father made a promise to the Son that He would be our priest forever. And then He confirmed it with an oath when He said, "The Lord has sworn and will not change his mind." (Hebrews 7:21)

That's good enough, don't you think?

For years I thought all people fell into one of two spiritual categories - they were lost or they were saved. They did not accept Jesus as their Savior or they had accepted Jesus as their Savior. Those were the only two options.

If they were lost, then they had no forgiveness and no hope for eternal life. Their understandable philosophy could only be to eat, drink, and be merry for tomorrow they would die.

But if they were saved, they had forgiveness - although it was conditional upon their frequent confession. They needed to know what God expected of them so that they could stay righteous and pleasing to God. They were dependent upon repentance and confession. They benefited from altar calls and confessional booths because they needed to ask for forgiveness.

I would now divide the second category – the saved – into two groups. Some live under a mixing of the Old Covenant with the New and some live under the New Covenant.

This latter group knows a finished and an unconditional forgiveness. They realize they are fully forgiven. And they live in thankfulness for that forgiveness. They don't need to continue seeking something they already have. They just enjoy it and rest in it.

CHAPTER TWELVE

PLEASING GOD

There is a billboard on Interstate Highway 20 that runs east and west through much of the state of Texas. I drive past that sign several times each year. And I never pass by it without grimacing.

The sign has now been there for ten or more years. It is a big billboard, double-sided and well-lit at night. Both sides have the same content. The message is in bold black print, "*You are God's child. Make Him proud.*"

I don't think the owner of the sign is directing his message to non-Christians. If he is, he has chosen a most ineffective approach. No, I think he is talking to Christians. And thousands drive by and read that sign every day, twenty-four hours each day, three hundred and sixty-five days a year.

What does that sign say to them? It confirms their belief that God is watching them. And He expects them to do good things. And He is proud of them *only when they do what He expects them to do.*

It that true? Is God proud of you only when you do good? Is His love that conditional?

What Does God Think Of Us?

God's love has never been conditional. Under the Old Covenant, man's righteousness was conditional, but God's love was constant. He never stopped loving Israel even though they were unfaithful to Him and His commandments. In fact, He gave them the Law so that they would realize their own need for a new righteousness. Even the Law was an expression of God's love.

And now we live under a New Covenant. If we have received the righteousness of Christ that counts on our behalf, then God sees us in that righteousness. Jesus has already received God's verdict: "*This is my Son in whom I am well pleased.*" And we are heirs of His Son's righteousness.

Because of our acceptance of the work of Christ, God has changed our status. He has made us holy. We are now blameless and without any blemish of unrighteousness. We are free from accusation. We are completely forgiven. We are righteous in God's sight.

> But now he has reconciled you by Christ's physical body through death to present you holy in his sight, without blemish and free from accusation..." (Colossians 1:22)

Some doubters might be quick to point out the verse which follows:

> ... if you continue in your faith, established and firm, not moved from the hope held out in the gospel. This is the gospel that you heard and that has been proclaimed to every creature under heaven, and of which I, Paul, have become a servant. (Colossians 1:23)

Does this verse say that we are holy in God's sight and free from accusation *as long as we continue* to be faithful? Is it instructing us to be established in our righteous works and to be firm in our goodness so that we can continue to be holy and free from accusation in God's sight?

No, Paul says we are holy and blameless *if we have a steadfast faith in the work of Christ.* We are without accusation if our hope is in the gospel. Specifically, our hope is in the gospel proclaimed by Paul – his gospel of a righteousness apart from the Law. We are to stand firm in that. That belief and acceptance opens us up to a new identity in God's eyes. That is our trust and hope. That is the gospel.

Our holiness is not contingent upon us. And we don't make God proud or not proud by what we do. We are holy because God says so. He has made us holy and blameless. He has made us righteous. We can stand firm in that knowledge.

Remember the name Chuck Colson? Chuck Colson was associated with Nixon and the Watergate episode in 1972. But many know him best for his conversion to Christ and his very productive evangelistic ministry in prisons and jails.

Colson sat down for an interview with Time Magazine in 2009. During that interview he expressed concerns about a trend he saw in churches:

> "The church has fallen into a therapeutic model. It believes its job is to make people happy and take care of their problems. It's a feel-good kind of Christianity. I don't think the job of the church is to make people happy. I think it's to make them holy."

Colson's interview with Time Magazine
Q&A: Religious Leader Chuck Colson
By Amy Sullivan Thursday, Sept. 24, 2009

Did Colson have it right? Is the work of the church to make people holy? That is true if holiness is seen as doing the right things. It would be true if we think we go to church to learn of our sin and learn what God expects of us. And since that is the majority view people have for the role of church participation, Colson's statement likely expresses many Christians' viewpoints.

But that is not God's view. Our holiness and righteousness are not created by church and Christian deeds. Our holiness is given to us by God. He has made us righteous.

I have a friend who has long attended a church in his community. As we talked one day, he expressed his pride in his church. His church has an outstanding musical program and well-designed activities for all ages. It is a thriving and growing church with a weekly attendance of almost four thousand participants. But those characteristics are only supplementary to my friend's main source of pleasure with his church.

He really likes his preacher. And he likes the preaching style. He told me a favorite and frequent statement that his preacher makes: "You are out in the world for six days between Sundays. You need this one day a week to get enough correction to last for those six days."

Is that the purpose of the church? To give attenders enough correction to last until they come back for more correction?

I visited recently with another friend who lives nearby. He told me how he had wanted to come hear me preach, but he first visited a church at an invitation from one of the members. He and his wife fell in love with that church. And again, this friend bragged on his preacher.

"I have never met a man who knew the Bible as well as he does," he remarked. "And, boy, can he be tough on us!"

Both of my friends are fine Christian men. But they both have missed out on the true origin of holiness and righteousness. They are striving to earn a righteousness with God and have failed to understand that righteousness comes only by God's grace.

Pleasing God

It is a natural response to God's character and His love for us that we would desire to please Him. But the question is, "How do we do that?"

Do we please Him by doing good works? We have already seen that He views our best works as filthy rags. So do we please Him by living righteous lives? He has already declared that there is not one single righteous person justified by works or good deeds. So is it possible to please Him?

There is actually only one way we can ever please God. And it often gets missed because it is not the way we might think. And it is not the way we have usually heard.

Since God has declared that we can never earn righteousness and since He has entered into a covenant by which we inherit the righteousness of Christ, the only way we can be pleasing to Him is to *accept* those truths. We agree that He is correct. We accept what God has said about our unrighteousness and the hopelessness of our making ourselves acceptable. We agree that we cannot attain righteousness. We see what God has done for us in giving us salvation and forgiveness. We receive the life of Christ into our lives.

In other words, we please God when we accept that what He did is necessary and that it is sufficient.

One day the disciples asked Jesus what it was that God required. What works were they to do? How could they satisfy God's expectations? How could they please Him?

And Jesus answered very clearly. He said there is only one thing God requires: Believe in the Savior.

> Then they asked him, "What must we do to do the works God requires?" Jesus answered, "The work of God is this: to believe in the one he has sent." (John 6:28-29)

Jesus did not give the disciples a list. And He did not remind them that they needed to be righteous and good so that God would be proud of them. But He did give them the true answer to their question. God wanted one thing: He wanted them to believe that His way of salvation was the only way.

So how do we please God? We please Him by admitting that we cannot please Him with our own performance. We please Him when we trust the righteousness He has given us. If we refuse that offer, we are ignoring the finished work of righteousness Christ accomplished on the cross.

So how do we please Him? We please Him by receiving what He has done for us.

I finished my Christmas shopping for my wife early this past year. It was relatively easy because every item I was considering was offered on the internet by multiple sellers. After some looking around, I decided to get her a diamond bracelet. I visited several jewelry websites and looked for the one I thought she would like. The item was then shipped to my front door. All of that was the easy part. The hard part was waiting for the time I could give Cheryl my gift. I was pleased with it, and I was anxious for her to see it. And my greatest pleasure came when she opened the box and expressed her happiness with it. It pleases me that she liked my gift. And it now brings me pleasure every time I see her wear it.

God has given us a gift that He Himself says we could never earn. No one could ever be good enough. No one could ever deserve His gift. So He gives it freely.

And what do we then do? We try to earn it. And we try to show Him we merit it. We try to make Him proud of how well we are doing.

But He is pleased by only one simple act. He is pleased when we admit our need and accept His gift.

Chapter Thirteen

Is Being a Christian Hard?

There was a bug struggling on the hardwood floor. I was seated in my favorite chair reading the newspaper when I looked down and saw that bug on its back. Its legs were in constant frantic motion as it was trying to turn over. But its ceaseless efforts had no effect. Nevertheless, it continued to struggle.

"Struggle" is a word that I often hear people use when they are describing the Christian life.

For a number of years I taught a group Bible study at a summer Christian camp. One year I asked a group of eleven to thirteen year-olds to write down questions that they would like to have answered. I will never forget one girl's question: "Why does being a Christian have to be so hard?"

We make being a Christian hard because we most typically attempt it with the Sin Management approach. We think that there are things that we are supposed to do. But then we can't do them well enough. Or we know that there are other things we are not supposed to do. And we find ourselves doing them. So we confess and rededicate and try harder. Holiness is a goal that we strive to attain – at least at some acceptable level. And if we are really honest about our struggling, we question: Why is it so hard?

Being a Christian is not hard. It is impossible.

Did you know that the world's best swimmers can swim one mile in under fifteen minutes? And the world record for swimming distance is almost one hundred and forty miles. Both are amazing accomplishments.

But what would happen if you met a world class distance swimmer on a Florida beach and asked him to swim to France? Would he make it? He might make it one hundred and forty miles further than I could, but he would not even come close. It would be impossible.

The problem with us trying to live a Christian life is that we have an erroneous idea of the standard required. We compare our own goodness to the goodness we see in others. But attaining or exceeding the goodness of others is not the goal. We are to be perfect as God is perfect. Holiness is not a diluted standard. It is not fifty-fifty. It is everything or nothing. Is reaching a perfect holiness hard? No, it is impossible. That would be an endless struggle.

So God made the impossible possible. But it was not a method we could accomplish in our own efforts. It was by His grace.

God's Formula For Godliness

The term *formula* often implies a step-by-step process. We do indeed hear of formulas for godliness and righteousness that rely upon a list of Christian disciplines that we can follow to live as a Christian is supposed to live.

But God has only one formula.

> His divine power has given us everything we need for life
> and godliness through our knowledge of him who called us
> by his own glory and goodness. Through these he has given
> us his very great and precious promises, so that through
> them you may participate in the divine nature and escape

the corruption in the world caused by evil desires. (2 Peter 1:3-4)

God tells us that He has given us everything we need for life and godliness. This is the very goal we are encouraged by religion to attain! And now God has given us everything we need to reach it. But it is not by our efforts, it is by His divine power.

This promised godliness is through our knowledge of Him. This is not referring to Bible knowledge or a knowledge of religious rules. It is not referring to knowing more about God. The knowledge is the understanding of God's own goodness and the truth of His calling us to believe His way of godliness and righteousness.

God has made us many great and precious promises. He has promised us a righteousness apart from the Law. He has promised that His Spirit will come and indwell us. He said that He would write His laws upon our hearts. And this was all done because of His mercy and grace. He has given us promises (through a New Covenant) because of His goodness and for His glory.

And God gives us a new heart. We are made new creations. Christ's Spirit lives in us and through us. And we are no longer slaves to our old nature, but we are now joined to His divine nature. This participation in the divine nature enables us with the power to escape corruption and evil desires.

The Sin Management approach says that we operate in our own power and efforts. It says that godliness is up to us and our choices. But the only way to overcome sin is not found in our own power. It can only be done through God's power operating within us.

So, back to our question. Why is living a Christian life so hard? It is because we don't understand and accept God's formula. His way is not about us, it is about Him. But we do try to make it about us. And we continue to struggle in our own power.

Saul Alinsky became famous for his successful organizational tactics for community organizing. His *Rules for Radicals* outlines strategies for community organizers to follow in uniting and empowering people to affect change by challenging the current agencies that promote social and economic inequality.

Here is his fourth rule:

> "*Make the enemy live up to their own book of rules.* You can kill them with this, for they can no more obey their own rules than the Christian church can live up to Christianity."
>
> Saul D. Alinsky
> *Rules for Radicals*
> New York: Random House, 1971
> page 128

I don't know what Saul Alinsky's religious background might or might not have been. But He did realize a significant weakness with a legalistic approach to Christianity. He knew that it is not possible to live up to a religion of rules.

Not a New Problem

The German priest and professor of theology, Martin Luther, was one of the foremost leaders of the Protestant Reformation of the 1500's. Through his personal study of the

Book of Romans he came to an awareness that the religious emphasis of the church of that day was in error. He concluded that righteousness by Law was clearly refuted by God's Word. And he saw the need for God's power working in a Christian's life.

> The Law says, "Do this," and it is never done. Grace says, "Believe in this," and everything is done.
>
> Martin Luther
> Cited in Gerhard O. Forde
> *On Being a Theologian of the Cross:*
> *Reflections on Luther's Heidelberg Disputation, 1518*
> Grand Rapids, MI: Eerdmans, 1997
> page 127

Martin Luther discovered that godliness and righteous living could never be attained by obeying the Law. The Law gave the proper commands, but those commands could never be fulfilled. But through his careful study of the Book of Romans, he realized that grace did make righteousness possible. He understood that grace says that we are to believe in God's way for godly living through His power. And Martin Luther realized that the grace approach was the only way true righteousness could ever be received.

Falling From Grace

Have you ever met someone who has fallen from grace? I have. And often you will find them gathering in churches and exhorting one another to do all the things Christians are supposed to do.

I will never forget raising my hand one afternoon in a seminary class being taught by a favorite professor. The semester class was on Paul's letter to the Galatians and we were discussing Galatians 5:4:

You who are trying to be justified by law have been
alienated from Christ; you have fallen away from grace.

When recognized by my professor, I pointed out that it seemed to me the scripture was not talking about being alienated from Christ and losing one's salvation because of sinful failures. Rather it was teaching exactly the opposite. It seemed to be saying that efforts to be justified by obeying God's Laws meant that one was placing trust in self-righteousness instead of in the work of Christ. Anyone who did that was not relying upon God's grace.

The professor paused and considered my statement for a moment before remarking that I had made an interesting comment. He then led the class in discussing whether the Bible gave any definite answers on what sins could result in someone losing salvation and falling out of God's grace.

I have looked back at that experience and wondered how the class missed the obvious point Paul stated. And then I realized. They believed and knew the truth about grace, but they were running it through long established filters.

Christians have long debated whether one can or cannot fall out of God's grace because of the commission of a certain quality or quantity of sins. But *alienated from Christ* does not refer to losing salvation. It means that one does not depend upon the finished work of Christ on his behalf. It means depending upon ourselves for righteousness. It means trying to mix grace and Law. It means we have fallen away from trusting in grace only.

Grace, But...

Sometimes, we add to the message of God's amazing grace even as we proclaim and sing about it. We believe in grace, but we add a comma and a preposition to it. We say, "Grace, but..." We believe it is grace plus faithfulness. Grace but also obedience. Grace but also good works.

We think that grace alone is too simple and it is not demanding enough. Perhaps it needs to be proven and kept by other works. Perhaps it needs our help.

I recently saw a message on the marquee sign in front of a church. The sign quoted 2 Timothy 2:1:

"Stay strong in the grace of the Lord."

I knew that particular church had a reputation for being very legalistic in its teachings, and I had that impression confirmed by a visit to the church's website. It cited the importance of obeying God's Law and even had the Ten Commandments listed on their homepage. So what was their reference to the grace of the Lord about?

In their view "staying strong" meant being disciplined and faithful. It was an encouragement to strive for godliness and righteous living. They were following the same interpretation that is common in many Christian teachings and churches. We are called to be strong and faithful. We believe in grace, but we add conditions to it. We say, "Grace, but..."

So what was Paul saying in his statement to Timothy? He was writing to encourage his young friend to stay strong in his dependence upon grace only. He instructed him to not let grace be filtered down or to have conditions added to it. He wanted Timothy to stay strong in the truth of grace.

It Is Not Just Hard, It Is Impossible

I was standing on a stage in front of almost six hundred very excited kids attending a Christian children's summer camp. I called a volunteer forward to draw a piece of paper out of a box. Every child in attendance had his or her name on a piece of paper in that box.

As the volunteer handed me a single strip of paper, I called out the name and invited the camper to join me on the stage. It was a girl. And she didn't know it yet, but she had already won a big screen television. It was a done deal.

The thrilled child came onstage and I announced that she would take home that big screen television by accomplishing one simple task. She only had to toss a rubber ball into the big box that had been placed at her feet.

Easy enough? But there were a few slight adjustments.

First, the box was moved about fifty feet away. And then, four adults were placed in front of the box to bat away her toss. Next, the contestant was blind-folded and turned around several times until she was completely disoriented.

With each new condition, she became less and less excited as she realized her task was becoming harder and harder. She then reached the point where she knew the requirement was completely hopeless. And the audience also knew that she was not going to win the prize. With each new "adjustment" to the game, they began to boo.

But then I announced an alternative option for her. If she wanted me to, I would place the ball in the box for her.

118

Of course she wanted me to! So I took the ball from her hands and walked across the stage. The adults blocking the box stepped aside as I calmly placed the ball in the box. And then the young girl was given her prize.

We played that game at camp for several years. The contestants changed and the size of the big screen television differed. But one thing remained the same. We always called that game by the same title.

The name of the game was *That's Grace*.

CHAPTER FOURTEEN
GRACE AND THE SIN PROBLEM

I know what you are thinking. And you are certainly not alone. It's the same thing almost everybody thinks.

If God has already forgiven all our sin – and if God has declared us holy and righteous in His sight – and if our forgiveness is finished – then what prevents us from sinning all we want? If God doesn't count our sins against us then what's the motivation to avoid it? Isn't grace a license to sin? Isn't it saying to just go right ahead? Will not grace remove the barriers and lead to more sin?

This is an interesting concern because I don't think anybody has actually ever needed a license to sin. It seems that every human has found that sin comes naturally enough. We don't seem to need instructions on how to sin. No, the general consensus seems to be that instructions are needed on how *to not* sin.

But this question of grace leading to more sinning is an expected one. And it has been around for a long time. Paul addressed it in Romans 6:1-2.

> "Shall we go on sinning so that grace may increase? By no means!"

Paul said that the idea of grace leading to sin was a false and preposterous idea. To claim that grace is a license to sin is a perversion of the truth, but more than that, it reveals a significant misunderstanding of what grace truly is.

Grace might promote sin if the reason a Christian doesn't sin is because he fears God's punishment. And it might promote sin if we are living godly lives because we are hoping for heavenly rewards.

So it is true that if someone sees Christianity as only a pardon for sins or a race for a bigger and better heavenly mansion, then it might be a concern that grace would promote sin. But if real Christianity and real grace means being transformed by the indwelling life of Christ, and if we are submitting to the Spirit of Christ living within us, we can't be comfortable living in sin.

Christians have developed numerous theories on why a relationship with God through Christ helps to overcome sin. Some say we now have a higher motivation because love for God is now our reason for obedience. We don't sin because we love God. We don't serve Him to gain His love, but we serve Him because He loves us. A realization of God's love leads us to a humble submission and obedience.

That sounds very good. And it sounds very spiritual. But it is not an approach that is ever going to bring consistent success. Love is a powerful motivation, but it is not strong enough to overcome a sinful nature. A human sinful nature is going to allow a love for God and for others, but it is never going to allow anything to overcome the dominant love for self. Love for self and interest in self might be temporarily muted, but that love for self will always eventually override our best intentions. We can't prevent it. It is our default setting.

Others say that a Christian can learn to resist sin because God is changing our hearts and our minds. He has enrolled us in a process of becoming increasingly holy. That also sounds very spiritual. But it still misses a key point.

The idea of God progressively changing our hearts and minds typically involves a none-too-subtle premise that we become more holy and resistant to sin by our own faithfulness to activities such as a daily prayer time, frequent Bible study, weekly worship and keeping our radio dial on Christian stations. The idea is based on the premise that we can learn how to successfully manage our sin.

These well-intentioned theories miss the point of what actually happens at our salvation. It is not that we are changed or that we begin to be changed. The actual truth is much superior to that. We are recreated. We become a new creation. It is not that our heart is changed. The truth is that we receive a new heart.

Romans 12:2 does speak of being transformed. But look at the verse more closely.

> Do not conform to the pattern of this world, but be
> transformed by the renewing of your mind. Then you will be
> able to test and approve what God's will is—his good,
> pleasing and perfect will.

Paul does call us to be transformed. But that transformation is based upon a *renewed* mind. It is not a transformation of self; it is a death to self. We can change our minds and we can refocus our minds. We can even redirect our minds. But no man can renew his own mind. That is a spiritual work that only God can do. We can only fail when we try self-transformation through the means of will power or dedication. This is why a working of God alone that gives us a new heart and new mind can be the only true way to transformed living.

Notice the statement about being able to test and approve God's good and perfect will. "Test" means to sort out and to recognize the right decision from among all the possibilities. "Approve" means to agree that God's way is the best way. These are not done by a reformed mind. These insights are possible only with a new mind.

A reformed mind allows (and even encourages) a work and action to be accomplished by man. It means that we need to try harder. It means that we need instruction and teachings that will help us identify God's way. We will also need motivations to choose God's way. A reformed mind can only lead to attempts to act differently. But a new mind means that we are remade into something different. That is why a new mind can come only by a work of God.

Susie taught me this. Susie was my pig that I raised and entered into hog shows at the fair back in my teenage years. I had trained Susie to walk beside me and to stand still when I gave her the signal. But Susie also had to look good for the judges. So to make her more appealing, I would apply a generous amount of *Lucky Tiger* hair oil to the hairs on Susie's back. She would look so nice and shiny and groomed! But there was a problem. Not long after my grooming attempts, Susie would inevitably lie down and roll over in the dirt. I would get angry, but Susie couldn't help it. She was a pig and pigs like to roll in the dirt – especially when some oil has been rubbed onto their backs. It was my fault for not understanding the nature of a pig. My training and attempts at reforming could not overcome that nature.

Man's problem is that we have a human nature. We don't need a reformed mind and a reformed nature. We need a new nature and a new mind.

Christians might agree with these Biblical truths but still miss the point because of the religious filters we have had impressed upon us. Yes, the Bible says that we are new creations in Christ. And yes, the Bible says that the old is gone and the new has come. But the messages received are that we need to overcome our sinful nature by commitment and rededication. We need to hide God's Word in our hearts so that we won't sin. We need to stay close to Him so that we won't be too close to the world. We need to give Him our hearts. We need to give Him our minds.

These all sound good and right, but they are only more religious filters that cause us to miss the truth that God has given us a new heart and a new mind. They are the filters that cause a Christian to question what happens if we no longer use the Bible as our guideline for living. Aren't the rules helpful? Don't they give us needed direction? Doesn't the Bible tell us what to do? Doesn't it give us insights and motivations to rise above our sinfulness?

The grace message says that the choice is quite simple. Do we need to be empowered by the commands in our Bibles or do we need to be empowered by the Holy Spirit?

It was not long after I started teaching the full message of grace that I had a man request an appointment. I will never forget his concern that my sermons were not telling him the specifics of what to do. "What are we supposed to do?", he asked. I answered, "Submit yourself fully to Christ and let His Spirit live through you." "But," he asked, "What am I supposed to do?" I repeated my statement, "Submit yourself to Christ and let His Spirit live through you." He only became more flustered, "But you are not telling me what I am *supposed* to do."

The Bible tells us in 2 Peter 1:3-4 why it is not up to us to do something.

> His divine power has given us everything we need for a godly life through our knowledge of him who called us by his own glory and goodness. Through these he has given us his very great and precious promises, so that through them you may participate in the divine nature, having escaped the corruption in the world caused by evil desires.

A godly life is made possible by God's empowering as He gives us everything we need for godly living. And that empowering is based upon great and precious promises. We can escape corruption and evil desires because of *our participation in the divine nature.* He has put to death our old nature. He has given us a new nature. He has given us a new mind and a new heart.

The concern that grace promotes sin reveals a very limited perspective of what the Bible teaches. It is this partial definition of grace that leads to several unfortunate fallacies. The common belief is that grace is all about salvation. But after salvation we are at least partially on our own.

Grace is more than just the way to forgiveness and acceptance by God. It is more than just God's love that led to Jesus' sacrifice on the cross. Those are important aspects, but they are not all of it. We need to have a more complete grasp of the whole picture.

Grace is *God's working in our lives to do what we cannot do ourselves.* We could not save ourselves from the penalty of our sin. So God did it. By His grace. We cannot deserve forgiveness. So God gave it. By His grace. We cannot live a godly life in our own power. So God gives us His power. By His grace. We cannot draw forth the strength to handle all the difficult times throughout the various stages of our lives. So God handles them. By His grace.

It is an unfortunate understanding to only see that grace relates to salvation. Grace relates to living. It relates to how we respond and how we think and how we live.

But, it is even bigger than that. Grace is not only a power for living; grace is the story of God's most amazing miracle.

When we think of God's great miracles we might mention creation or the parting of seas. We might think of God's enabling a child to defeat a giant or of God's stopping the sun in the sky. We might think of great crowds being fed with only a little boy's lunch or of a few spoken words calming a storm. All are truly amazing miracles of God's power.

But the most amazing miracle is that God loved us and gave us new spiritual life. He justified us and declared us holy. And then, *He comes and lives in us.*

I know that people sing at Easter about a risen Savior living in our hearts and I know that they read about it in the Bible, but it has been my experience that a very small minority truly realizes what it means and how it applies.

The Bible says that Christ lives in us. He is not with us or watching over us. We do not go to meet Him in church buildings or prayer closets. He is in us. He lives His life *in* us and *through* us.

> "I have been crucified with Christ and I no longer live, but Christ lives in me." (Galatians 2:20)

"But if Christ is in you, your body is dead because of sin, yet your spirit is alive because of righteousness. And if the Spirit of him who raised Jesus from the dead is living in you, he who raised Christ from the dead will give life to your mortal bodies through his Spirit, who lives in you." (Romans 8:10-11)

This is the bigger picture of grace and salvation. Yes, Christ gave His life *for* us, but now He gives His life *to* us. We now have the Way and the Truth and the Life living in us. We are transformed by Him and now abide in Him and exhibit His fruit in our lives.

This is the reality of grace-living revealed in the Bible. And what are we *supposed* to do? We are to submit to Him and let Him live through us.

Think a moment about the image in the Bible of the potter and his clay. Isaiah (64:8) reminds man that he is only the clay; God is the potter. Therefore, we are the works of God's hands. God has His role. Man has his.

It is not up to the clay to purify itself. It is not the role of the clay to determine what kind of vessel it wishes to become. And it is certainly not the role of the clay to make something of itself! What is the role of the clay? The clay is to lay there until the potter picks it up. Then the potter makes what he decides to create.

Have you ever heard it said that we are God's hands and God's feet? No, we aren't. We are God's gloves and God's shoes. He indwells and fills us. He lives in us.

The choice is deciding between "Do I do it for Him?" or "Does His Spirit do it through me?" "Am I living for Him or is He living in me?" That is the difference between religious

Christianity and real Christianity. It is the difference between legalism and real Christianity.

The religious leaders of Jesus' day said, "Live for God." Jesus said, "I am God come to live in you." And they missed it.

As a child, I didn't know a lot about science or astronomy, but I did know that I could look up at night and see the moon. And I could see that the moon was giving off a light. Some nights the light from the moon was so bright that it even lit up my bedroom. But then later I learned that the moon produces no light at all. It has no light of its own. It is only reflecting the light from the unseen sun.

I also used to believe that I was supposed to shine for God. But then I learned that I have no light of my own. I am only to let the Son show and shine through me.

No. Grace is not a license to sin and grace does not promote sin. Grace is God working in our lives to give us a new heart and new life. Divine grace is everything we need for godliness and living. Grace is God's choice to indwell our lives and to shine through us.

CHAPTER FIFTEEN

TRUE GRACE

If many Christians have an incomplete definition of grace, then what exactly is the true grace of God?

The book of 1 Peter was written to Christians to help them understand concepts of holiness, faith in Christ, suffering under persecution, marriage relationships, defending the gospel, living for God and other aspects of the Christian life. Then at the end of that writing Peter stated his overall reason for his letter. He wrote that his purpose was to illuminate the true grace of God.

> "I have written to you briefly, encouraging you and testifying that this is the true grace of God. Stand fast in it." (1 Peter 5:12)

The Apostle Paul's gospel was also a message of God's grace. He dedicated his life to sharing the truth about grace in a world that was grounded in legalistic and works-based religions. Because of his message, he met much resistance and rejection from the religious system of his day. He was frequently imprisoned and suffered many other hardships. But he found that his grace message was bearing spiritual fruit.

> "All over the world this gospel is bearing fruit and growing, just as it has been doing among you since the day you heard

it and understood God's grace in all its truth." (Colossians 1:6)

What did Paul and Peter teach about grace? What is the "true grace of God"? What is "God's grace in all its truth?"

True grace is 100% pure grace.

True grace has to be pure. It cannot be mixed with human effort because human effort is the very reason we need grace. Grace cannot even be connected to human effort. If grace means unmerited favor, then you no longer have true grace if you start adding conditions of merit. When you add any element of human effort, grace is no longer grace.

This is the point that Paul made in his letter to the Christians at Rome.

> "And if by grace, then it is no longer by works; if it were, grace would no longer be grace." (Romans 11:6)

Mixing grace and works is like putting a few ounces of blue dye into a gallon of pure clean water. The water is no longer pure clean water. It may be mostly pure clean water. But it is not pure; it has been diluted. And what happens when you put a cup of blue dye into the water? What if you mix half water and half dye?

It might seem logical to think that our efforts affect whether God is pleased with us or disappointed with us or happy with us or mad at us. But grace is God's working in our lives based on His love - not our merit. If there is only one iota of our effort or merit, it is not true and pure grace. When you dilute it down at all, you no longer have grace.

Paul understood that any dependence upon works means an abandonment of grace. He warned that attempts to be justified by law are rejections of a dependence upon the saving work of Christ.

> "It is for freedom that Christ has set you free. Stand firm, then, and do not let yourselves be burdened again by a yoke of slavery. You who are trying to be justified by law have been alienated from Christ; you have fallen away from grace." (Galatians 5:1, 4)

Law and grace cannot be mixed because they are opposed to one another. They cancel one another out. Completely. One puts the effort or at least part of the effort upon us. The other puts all of the effort (and credit) upon God.

The very most simple definition of Law is "do." And the very most simple definition of grace is "done." We have religious pressures to do, but grace says that God has already done it all for us. We seek God's favor and acceptance. Law says do; grace says done. We desire God's forgiveness. Law says do; grace says done. We strive for holiness in God's eyes. Law says do; grace says done. We seek to attain righteousness. Law says do; grace says done.

Any attempts to combine the two ideas of "do" and "done" result in a diluted grace. "Done" cannot be added to. It is complete and finished. It is past tense. Grace must be pure and complete and sufficient or it is not true grace. True grace is 100% pure grace.

True grace extends past the initial gift of salvation.

The idea that grace is related to salvation alone is a very common error that misses the understanding of true grace as revealed in the Bible. We are familiar with the musical refrain of "Amazing grace that saved a wretch like me." We readily acknowledge that we could not save ourselves and we celebrate that we are saved by God's grace. But we often have the idea that God did it for us up to the point of our accepting Christ's salvation, but we are to pick it up from there as we live out our salvation. Bob George points out the troubling application of this error:

> "People are attracted to Christ by the message of His total love and acceptance and of salvation by grace; then, once they're in the family of God, they are leveled by demands for performance and conformity."

"Salvation" has been limited in our religious vocabulary as referring to our initial acceptance of Christ and the issue of where we go when we die. Here and now, however, the majority view is that God accepts you on the basis of performance.

This is not a new problem. Paul addressed the same error when he wrote what many scholars believe is his first letter of encouragement and instruction.

> "You foolish Galatians! Who has bewitched you? I would like to learn just one thing from you: Did you receive the Spirit by observing the law or by believing what you heard? Are you so foolish? After beginning with the Spirit, are you now

trying to attain your goal by human effort?" (Galatians 3:1-3)

Paul linked the unbreakable connection between the work of the Holy Spirit before and after salvation. Just as our salvation begins with the work of God's Spirit, it continues with the work of the same Spirit. Just as our salvation begins with grace, the living of the Christian life continues in that grace. The truth is that we enter into a relationship with God by grace; and we live in that relationship by grace.

When grace is limited to the love of God and the work of God in providing the sacrificial death of Christ for our sins, it is reduced from its full application. Grace also applies to God's powerful working in our lives. True spiritual living is His working in our lives, not our working for Him. Grace is the one word that encompasses all that God does for us both before and after our initial salvation. It comprises everything He does for us through Christ Jesus.

We see the benefits of grace *beyond* our initial salvation in Paul's writing to Titus:

> "For the grace of God that brings salvation has appeared to all men. It teaches us to say 'No' to ungodliness and worldly passions, and to live self-controlled, upright and godly lives in this present age." (Titus 2:11-12)

Grace is the basis of our salvation from the eternal penalty of sin, but it also has an additional role. It teaches us to say "no" to ungodliness. It is grace that not only teaches us to live godly lives, but gives us the spiritual power to live godly lives. Salvation certainly is by true grace. But true grace is more than just that initial salvation.

True grace is to be held onto adamantly.

What would the Apostle Paul say if he were to write to us today about the common combining of grace and works? How would he respond to the mixing of religious works with the purity of God's grace? Would he warn that the dilution of grace is a serious issue?

We can be assured that his stance would be the same today as it was when he wrote to the Christians in Galatia. He was very clear in his feelings. In fact, he repeated himself for emphasis:

> But even if we or an angel from heaven should preach a gospel other than the one we preached to you, let them be under God's curse! As we have already said, so now I say again: If anybody is preaching to you a gospel other than what you accepted, let them be under God's curse! (Galatians 1:8-9)

Not only was Paul perplexed about the "foolish Galatians" who were being "bewitched" (Galatians 3:1), but he recognized the grave danger contained in the false teachings. Just a few verses later in the chapter he would expand on his desire that the false teachers might be cursed as he warned that the people themselves were actually the ones being placed under a curse.

> For all who rely on the works of the law are under a curse, as it is written: "Cursed is everyone who does not continue to do everything written in the Book of the Law." (Galatians 3:10)

Why are we to take the combining of works and grace seriously? Why do we have to insist that grace not be diluted? Why do we have to abhor any teaching that emphasizes obedience through our human efforts for obtaining any measure of acceptance or righteousness in God's eyes? It is because when we give people a list of do's and don'ts, the Bible says we are putting them under a curse. We are setting them up to fail and to live in bondage. The Bible itself clearly warns that when we tell people to manage their sin, we are putting them under a curse.

It is an unimaginable deed in our culture today to place a curse upon someone. We associate that type of action with superstitious or even evil beliefs. But Paul says that our churches are doing that very thing when they promote a mixing of grace with Law. That's how serious it is. That is why we have to hold onto true grace adamantly.

True grace will be welcomed... by some.

The truth of pure and unfiltered grace would seem to be a wonderful message to all who hear it, but in reality some are uncomfortable with what they perceive as an over-emphasis upon grace. They fear (perhaps unconsciously) that if it is all about what God does and nothing at all about what we do, then we have lost any degree of control over the whole situation. That does not seem fair or logical. God's opinion of us should at least be affected to some degree by our goodness and efforts!

And the grace message certainly goes against the status quo and the sin management emphasis that has been taught to us for our entire Christian lives. Plus, will not an acceptance of the grace message promote and even encourage sin?

These ideas explain why so many sincere Christians are uncomfortable and express warnings about too much emphasis upon grace. But for those who begin to understand it, it is a message of freedom and joy.

And as we have seen earlier, the Apostle Paul witnessed the positive effects of people receiving the message of grace:

> "All over the world this gospel is bearing fruit and growing, just as it has been doing among you since the day you heard it and understood God's grace in all its truth." (Colossians 1:6)

Paul's personal awareness of the positive acceptance of the grace message is even more insightful when we consider the context of his experiences. He lived in a world that focused upon religious pathways to God's favor. And time and time again that religious world resisted his gospel of grace. But where his gospel was being accepted, it was spreading among the people who were understanding the full picture of God's pure grace.

A resistance to unfiltered grace is still occurring today. Religion is too often defined by rules and "do's and don'ts." Since true grace cannot co-exist with those established teachings, the grace message is not welcomed by everybody. It can only be accepted in a very diluted form. But for those who do receive it, it is joy and peace and rest as we realize that we have peace with God. We are justified entirely. And we realize that God's evaluation of us is based upon the grace to which Christ Jesus has given us access.

Our souls rest in gladness as we understand the words of the former legalist himself:

> Therefore, since we have been justified through faith, we have peace with God through our Lord Jesus Christ, through whom we have gained access by faith into this grace in which we now stand. And we boast in the hope of the glory of God. (Romans 5:1-2)

We now have true peace with God. And we rest in the grace to which we have been given access.

CHAPTER SIXTEEN

BELIEVING IN UNFILTERED GRACE

The message of unfiltered grace is met with a variety of responses. Many will claim it to be a false teaching that distorts Biblical truth. Some will warn that it is misleading. It will be seen as radical. Or it will be viewed as an easy out that exaggerates God's love and mercy. Some will claim that it is only wishful thinking by people who are not serious about sin. Or they will warn that it is irresponsible because it nullifies the value of Christian commitment.

Are these opinions true? Or is the grace message the true and consistent teaching of God's Word that is to be taken at face value? Does it remove the distortions of human logic? Is it pushing through the religious add-ons and returning to the original pure gospel?

There is only one reliable source of truth – God's Word. And there is only one reliable teacher of that truth – the Holy Spirit. God alone can fill us with wisdom and spiritual understanding (Colossians 1:9). God alone can make known to us the mysteries of His will which He purposed for us in Christ (Ephesians 1:9). And we know that no man can conceive of the truths of God unless they are revealed to us by the Holy Spirit (1 Corinthians 2:9-10).

Open your heart and mind to that Spirit. Ask Him to reveal truth to you. Set aside your opinions or preconceived beliefs and ask Him to teach you. Ask Him to enable you to take down the filters of past teachings and human reasoning.

And ask Him to guard you against mixing any shadow of Law with true grace. Choose whether you will relate to God through your own righteousness or through His grace. You can't do both. And choose whether you will rely upon the works of self or the work of Christ. Again, you can't do both.

It is understandable that we desire to know what it takes to please God. Or at least we want to know how we are to try. Fortunately we can know the answer because we have the Biblical record of that very question being asked to Jesus by the disciples. And we have Jesus' response.

> "Then they asked him, 'What must we do to do the works God requires?' Jesus answered, 'The work of God is this: to believe in the one he has sent.'" (John 6:28-29)

The disciples wanted to know the bottom-line answer. What was it that God wanted them to do? What did He require? They probably expected a list of works that they were responsible to accomplish. But Jesus' answer was very clear and concise. He said that God required one thing. God wants you to believe. That's not just referring to an intellectual head belief - for even the demons do that. No, it means to rely and depend upon what Jesus has done for you. It means to depend upon Him for righteousness and to depend upon Him for holiness. It means to put all of your eggs into that one basket.

Religion teaches us to behave. Grace teaches us to believe. We are to believe that Jesus has fulfilled the covenant of righteousness and that God has made us the spiritual heirs of His work. God has given the righteousness of Christ to us.

Believe in what Christ has done for you. Allow His Spirit to animate your spirit and to live through you. Remember that we are not changed; we are new creations. We are now righteous and blameless. We are without fault and free from accusation. We are holy and indwelt by Christ's Spirit.

Let Him do through you what He wants to do. That's all. He just wants you to do that. He wants you to receive and to live in His grace – without the religious filters.

Chapter Seventeen

Preaching Grace

The pastor on the other end of the phone was a personal friend. As soon as he began speaking I could hear in his voice that he was troubled. I soon learned why. He was calling me with a concern for one of our mutual personal friends. He was worried about Neal.

Neal was the chairman of deacons and a Bible Study teacher at the church my friend had previously pastored. A good man and a popular Bible teacher, Neal had gotten off track. He had rejected some of his previous beliefs and was insisting on teaching heresy and unbiblical ideas. He had been removed from teaching and was becoming increasingly uninvolved with the church.

My pastor friend was concerned. Knowing I had a relationship with Neal, he asked me if I would go by and help Neal see the error of his new ideas.

Neal and his wife graciously welcomed me into their home. In fact, Neal was quite anxious to talk to me about theology and Bible doctrine. Over the next hour I learned Neal was not interested in being shown his unbiblical beliefs. But he was very interested in sharing his new beliefs with me. Towards the conclusion of our visit, Neal went into an adjoining room and took a book out of a box. It was clear he had dozens of copies. "Read this," he said. "It will explain what I've been talking about."

I went home and began to thumb through the book. The book Neal had given me was *Classic Christianity* by Bob George. The introduction talked about rediscovering "the real thing." Warning bells went off in my head as soon as I read the phrase. It sounded very vain and even cultish to declare that one was writing a book to help Christians discover the *real* thing.

Getting out a note pad to keep a list of the unbiblical and false ideas, I began reading. And I continued to read "just one more chapter" until late into the night. After finishing each chapter, I would conclude, "There's nothing wrong with that. Those are clearly the teachings of scripture. Maybe the next chapter will be obviously false."

The next morning I finished the book. I had my list, but it was not falsehoods I would use to confront Neal. It was the realization and applications of wonderful and exciting Biblical teachings that I wanted to share with my congregation.

Looking back, I see that God had already planted seeds of grace in my life, but in the hours spent reading that book, God opened up my heart and His Spirit revealed a fuller picture of grace and spiritual life than I had ever realized.

I immediately began teaching and preaching grace, although I was still unable to let go of some of my earlier conditioning. I still held onto fragments of the old which I attempted to incorporate into the new. The grace message was run through the filters of my years of religious training.

Developing a bigger picture of grace has been a process. Actually, it still is. But God is continuing to show me a fuller understanding of grace. I now see it everywhere in scripture. There have been disappointments along the way as I have found that many Christians believe in the concept of grace but just don't realize what it means. Many don't even agree with what it means. Even more often, they run it through their own religious filters. The message is heard, but it is nicely fit into the beliefs they have always been taught. They will sing about grace and quote verses about it, but when they begin to hear it more fully taught, they become uncomfortable. I have had church visitors stand up and walk out during the sermon. Several members left our church and shared with other churches that I had gone off course. But many others caught it. Or, I guess I should say that grace caught them.

My journey is a joyful and restful one. Over the past dozen years I have seen the grace message being taught in ever-widening circles. A glance at the bookstore shelves or the online book sellers indicates the increasing interest. There used to be a few books by a few authors. Now there are many insightful books and websites presenting the grace message. Some are suggesting that we are even seeing signs of a new reformation within Christianity. People are writing about real grace and reading about grace and seeking churches where unfiltered grace is taught. Warning bells go off and they have a discomfort when they hear grace and self-righteousness joined together.

But let me warn you. Preaching an unfiltered grace message will probably cost you. Faithful church members will not like the idea that they cannot take pride in their own righteousness. Some will leave to find a church that gives them a list. Members you cherish as friends will begin to say that you are promoting sin.

I remember insightful counsel that one of my "grace mentors" gave me when I was at a particularly low point. It sounds highly sacrilegious that we should ever compare our troubles to Christ's suffering, but my friend reminded me that Jesus was crucified by the religious leaders of His day for preaching a message of grace instead of Law.

So, hear this warning. But ask God's Spirit to open your heart and mind to the truth of grace. Read the Bible in its full context and see the consistent emphasis on grace and life in Christ.

Begin to live in it yourself. Rest in it.

And teach the truth to others. Let the truth set them free. Help them see the pure grace message.

Unfiltered.

STUDY GUIDE

GRACE... MADE TO FIT

1. What is your definition of grace?

2. Has your understanding of grace been adjusted or revised by religious filters? How?

3. The author identifies several areas in which Christians reveal they are not resting in complete grace. Which ones do you identify with?

4. What does the author mean by "sin management"? Have you experienced this approach? How common do you think it is?

5. What does the author mean by relying upon human faithfulness to accomplish good works? Is anything wrong with this? If so, what?

6. What do you think Jesus was teaching in his metaphor of new wine being poured into old wineskins? What is the new wine? What is represented by the old wineskins?

7. What did you like about the author's definition of grace? What did you dislike?

LAW: GOOD OR BAD?

1. What are some positive benefits of the Law?

2. Why does the author refer to people of the Old Testament as law attempters? What examples can you think of demonstrating that this is true?

3. Were you surprised by the explanation of the purpose of the Law? Is that the way you have seen it? Is it the way most Christians see it? Why?

4. How did the Pharisees of Jesus' day view the Law? How did they reach that point of understanding?

5. Define and describe legalism. Does it exist today? How?

6. How did Paul receive his understanding of the gospel? What were the advantages of this? What were the disadvantages?

7. How does the Law condemn?

8. The author described a strategy sometimes used to help youth avoid premarital sex. What is good about that approach? What is bad?

RELIGIOUS BEHAVIOR MODIFICATION

1. How effective do you think behavior modification is? How effective is spiritual behavior modification? Why or why not?

2. The author mentioned several motivations for following laws. Which are the most motivational for you? Of those cited, which is the most common motivator in your opinion?

3. Why do religious laws need constant refining and redefining? Can you cite an example of this being done?

4. If the failure rate of obeying the Law is 100%, why do we continue to set ourselves up for failure?

5. Is sin management helpful or harmful? Explain your answer.

6. Is the Law good or bad? Explain your answer.

7. Do you relate to the man mentioned in the final part of the chapter? If so, in what ways?

A New Way

1. How does the imagery of "missing the mark" apply to the concept of sin? How consistent are you in hitting the mark? How do you feel about that?

2. What are the differences between our working for God and God doing His work through us? Which do you believe is God's intended approach?

3. The author outlined how some Biblical writers recognized the futility of man earning righteousness. Which example was the most insightful to you? Why do some Christians today not acknowledge the same futility?

4. Compose a one sentence summary of the teaching presented in Romans 3:10, Romans 3:20, Galatians 2:21b and Philippians 3:8-9.

5. What do you believe was the key point of Jesus' first recorded sermon?

6. How is the gospel "good news"?

7. Why is the sin management approach so popular today? The author mentioned two results of the method. Which do you believe is the most common? Which is the greatest danger to you personally?

8. Do you agree with the validity of the two courtroom scenarios presented in the chapter? Why or why not?

9. For deeper thought: Matthew 7:13-14 recounts Jesus speaking of two roads. When we read those verses in the context of the teaching we see that Jesus was addressing the Pharisees and their idea of righteousness by works. Is Jesus talking about the road to heaven and the road to hell? That's the application we've always heard. Or is He talking about two roads men take trying to get to righteousness? One road is paved by human efforts and strivings to follow the Law. The journey down that road results in bondage and condemnation or false pride. The other road is the true way of righteousness. The journey down that narrow road is a journey of grace and forgiveness and life. Which truth do you think Jesus was addressing?

SALVATION OR RIGHTEOUSNESS?

1. What do you understand to be the distinction between forgiveness and righteousness?

2. Why does Paul cite a righteousness *from* God? What is Paul's point in Romans 3 regarding boasting?

3. Do you feel "expiation" or "propitiation" are more accurate terms than "atonement"? Why or why not?

4. In your opinion, are there levels of reward in heaven? What would be the advantages of such a system? What would be the fallacy of such a system?

5. How would the capacity for Christians to lose their righteousness make God inconsistent?

6. Are Christians "sinners saved by grace"? Explain your answer.

7. After reading the summary of *America's Four Gods*, which view of God does your closest non-Christian friend hold? Which view was the predominant view taught in your childhood church?

8. What does it mean to be a "temple of God"? What is the sin management application? What is the grace application?

9. Which is true in your opinion: Is a believer only saved from the penalty of his sins committed before salvation or is he perfectly righteous in God's eyes?

RIGHTEOUSNESS MADE CERTAIN

1. Have you been warned of the judgment scenario described in the opening paragraphs of this chapter? What were/are your feelings about the scenario?

2. How does guilt affect the health of a relationship? Explain your answer.

3. How does guilt affect a relationship with God? What guilt have you experienced in your relationship with God?

4. How does the understanding that God has taken away the Christian's guilt affect a relationship with Him?

5. The author mentioned four theological words. Have you heard them mentioned before? Have you previously understood the meaning of the terms? How does each one impact your awareness of your righteousness?

6. What is your response to the chapter's statement that we are as righteous as Jesus Christ? Is this blasphemous? Confusing? False? True?

FINISHED FORGIVENESS

1. With which of the two Joe's do you most identify? Why? Which situation do you believe is the most common?

2. The author mentioned several objections to the teaching of finished forgiveness. What is your response to the following objections?

   Objection: That's not what I've been taught.
   Objection: It's not about lost relationship; it's about lost fellowship.
   Objection: I just feel better when I cover all my bases.

3. The most common objection to the concept of finished forgiveness is that it is contradictory to the teaching of the Bible. Respond to the author's interpretations of:

   James 5:16
   Luke 11:4
   1 John 1:9

4. Do you agree or disagree with the concept of finished forgiveness? Explain your answer. Has your opinion changed after reading this chapter?

COMPLETED RIGHTEOUSNESS

1. What is the distinction between *acting* holy and *being* holy? Which can we accomplish ourselves? Which can only God create? What are the ramifications of your answers?

2. What does Colossians 1:22 and 2 Corinthians 5:21 say about our identity in Christ?

3. What loopholes can be found in "all" and "once for all"? Do some find loopholes in these absolutes? Explain your answer. Why do you think this occurs?

4. How does Christ impact the Old Covenant sacrificial system?

5. Do you personally agree that the Bible teaches a finished forgiveness? If so, what is the most persuasive argument to you?

6. Does it hurt to keep asking God for forgiveness? What does it reveal?

THE BROKEN COVENANT

1. What is God's dividing line in history? Why?

2. What were the specifics of God's covenant with Abraham?

3. Work through the steps of God's communicating the Law to the children of Israel. How many times were they presented the demands of the Law? How many times did they promise to keep it? What was the outcome?

4. Are you surprised by the people's intentions, promises and eventual failure? Explain your answer.

5. How does the standard of "Be perfect as your heavenly Father is perfect" match up with man's adherence to God's Law?

6. What do you think Jesus was referring to when He gave this command? Was He setting up a required standard or a hopeless goal? What are the implications of each possibility? Explain your answers.

7. What was God's response to man's failure to fulfil the Law Covenant?

A New System for Righteousness

1. From which tribe of Israel did Jesus descend? Is this significant? If so, why?

2. Do you agree or disagree that the New Covenant bypassed man and was between God and Jesus? Have you heard or considered this idea before? Why would this be significant?

3. What point do you think Paul was making in Galatians 3:16?

4. How do Jesus' words at the Last Supper relate to the New Covenant?

5. How do Jesus' final three spoken words on the cross relate to the New Covenant?

6. How does the tearing of the temple curtain at the exact moment of Jesus' death relate to the New Covenant?

A SUPERIOR WAY

1. In what ways is Jesus a superior priest? What is the significance of each of those superior attributes?

2. In what ways did Jesus offer a superior sacrifice?

3. What is the one essential variance between the Old Covenant and the New Covenant? Why is this difference significant?

4. What do you think of when you hear of someone being put under a curse? Why does Paul say the Law puts men under a curse? What is your reaction to that statement?

5. Why is the new system possible to keep?

6. Is there a difference between God's Law and God's laws? Is so, what is the difference?

7. (From the author's illustration) How are Joseph and Joe similar? How are they different?

8. By which covenant system do you want to live? Why?

9. What do you think about the author's thoughts on spiritual categories? Do you agree or disagree? How strongly? Explain your answer. If you do agree, then which category do you fall into? Has this always been the case?

PLEASING GOD

1. Is God proud of you? Why or why not? Has your answer changed since reading this book? How?

2. What do you think are the most common reactions by those who have passed by the billboard mentioned in the introduction to this chapter?

3. Why was even the Law an expression of God's unconditional love? Do you agree that this is true? Explain your answer.

4. Do you agree or disagree with the author's interpretation of Colossians 1:23? Why or why not?

5. Do you believe that making people holy is the job of the church? Explain your answer. How common is this idea? Why do you think many Christians believe this to be true?

6. Do you agree that giving enough correction to last a week is the purpose of gospel preaching? Explain your answer. Have you ever held this opinion?

7. Why do you desire to please God? According to the author, how do we please God? Do you agree or disagree?

IS BEING A CHRISTIAN HARD?

1. As you look back upon your own experience, have you struggled to live the Christian life? In what ways have you found the Christian life hard to live?

2. What is God's formula for godliness? What is your response to that truth? How common is that emphasis in the beliefs of most Christians? What is the more common emphasis?

3. Why do you think Saul Alinsky used the church as an illustration in his fourth rule? What does that say about his view of the church? Do you think he was correct or incorrect?

4. What do you think about Martin Luther's statements? How well do you think those statements were received in his day? How are they received today?

5. Do you ever fall from grace? Explain your answer.

6. What conditions are sometimes added to the grace life?

GRACE AND THE SIN PROBLEM

1. Under what two beliefs does the author suggest an understanding of grace might promote sin? Why would this be true?

2. What are some common motivations for overcoming sin?

3. Why does self transformation ultimately fail? How has God remedied this problem?

4. What is the difference between a reformed mind and a new mind?

5. What are some of the religious filters that cause us to miss the truth that God has given us a new heart and a new mind?

6. Do we need to be empowered by the commands found in the Bible or by the Holy Spirit? Why?

7. What are some of the ways that unfiltered grace relates to more than initial salvation?

8. Do you personally believe that Jesus lives in you? In your understanding, what does that mean? What change of perspective has this created for you?

9. What do you think is the central point of the potter and his clay metaphor?

10. What is the difference between being God's hands/feet and being God's gloves or shoes? Is it a distinction worth making? Why or why not?

TRUE GRACE

1. Why does grace have to be 100% pure?

2. Do you agree with the simple definitions of Law ("do") and grace ("done")? Why or why not? Is this actually simple or is it complex? Explain your answer.

3. How have you experienced Christians being leveled by demands for performance or conformity? Explain your answer.

4. How does limiting grace to the love of God and the work of God in providing the sacrificial death of Christ for our sins reduce its full application?

5. Why must we insist that grace not be diluted in teachings and understandings? What is the harm?

6. Why do some Christians not welcome the message of true grace?

BELIEVING IN UNFILTERED GRACE

1. What responses to the message of unfiltered grace would you anticipate? Why do you think people have these responses?

2. According to the author, how can we learn spiritual truth?

3. Why is it so important to open our hearts and our minds to the Holy Spirit?

4. Why can't we rely upon both our own works and the work of Christ?

5. What was Jesus' bottom line answer for what God requires of us? What does this mean?

6. How has your definition and understanding of true grace changed after reading this book?

EASTER PRESS

Easter Press is the first outreach of a much larger vision of the Gospel Commune. Our purpose is to assist Christian authors in getting their books into the hands of those who need them.

> *"My heartfelt gratitude goes to Bill and Joanna with Easter Press for their support. They were sent to me at a time when it was most critical for the production of my book."*
>
> Jack Spiers, Author
> *I'll Ride My White Horse Again*

Our goal is to remove the financial and technical hurdles which have traditionally hindered new Christian authors from becoming published and spreading the Gospel of Jesus Christ.

If you have a manuscript which you would like to submit for consideration, please visit our website at www.EasterPress.com.

"...We are the Easter people and hallelujah is our song."
    – Pope John Paul II

Made in the USA
Monee, IL
18 May 2021